D0820683

APR

# Spectacular Bid

# Spectacular Bid

*by* TIMOTHY T. CAPPS

THOROUGHBRED
Legends®
No. 9

EP
ECLIPSE
PRESS

Lexington, Kentucky

Library of Congress Card Number: 00-108854

ISBN 1-58150-057-2

Printed in The United States
First Edition: May 2001

a division of
The Blood-Horse, Inc.
PUBLISHERS SINCE 1916

To learn more about Spectacular Bid
and other classic Thoroughbreds, see:

**www.thoroughbredlegends.com**

# SPECTACULAR BID

# CONTENTS

# INTRODUCTION

## *"The greatest horse..."*

H is trainer, always on good terms with hyperbole, called him "the greatest horse ever to look through a bridle" and often compared him to American Thoroughbred racing's ultimate icons — Man o' War, Citation, and Secretariat — with those horses sometimes taking the worst of it.

He would be remembered as a legitimate superstar in a decade (the 1970s) that produced more universally acclaimed great ones than any other in the history of the sport. When *The Blood-Horse* magazine published its list of the top 100 racehorses of the 20th century in 1999, he was ranked tenth, and three of the horses ahead of him — Secretariat (second), Forego (eighth), and Seattle Slew (ninth) — were all part of the '70s scene, as was Affirmed (twelfth).

To be mentioned in the same breath with three Triple

Crown winners was high praise indeed, but Spectacular Bid's admirers felt their horse might have been underrated. Not only by *The Blood-Horse* panel of racehorse evaluators, but underrated by latter-day commentators of the era who often tend, however understandably, to rate a sweep of the American Triple Crown races as deserving of the seat just to the right hand of God, at least the equine version thereof.

Comparisons of great racehorses, as with human athletes, are as fruitless as they are fun, but are fundamental to the racing fan's enjoyment of the game and an important element of a sport whose past is integral to its present and future.

If Spectacular Bid's fans are not satisfied with their hero's ranking, they can take comfort in another compilation done by English writers Tony Morris and John Randall in *A Century of Champions*, published by Portway Press Limited, which also publishes the authoritative and widely respected Timeform publications.

Since 1947, Timeform has produced both in-season and annual ratings of horses racing in Europe, primarily England and Ireland, that have become a standard worldwide. Created by the late Phil Bull in the 1930s

for his own handicapping purposes, the Timeform ratings are based, in part, on weight carried, distance,
winning or beaten distance (lengths), and time, with
ratings expressed in pounds. For reference purposes,
the highest year-end rating ever given to a horse was
Sea-Bird's 145 in 1965. An average English classic winner would rate in the low 130s, and horses above that
level are considered truly exceptional.

Morris and Randall rated the 200 best horses of the
20th century worldwide, clearly an ambitious task, but
one they obviously relished.

It took at least a 134 rating to make their "World Top
200." (Their view, shared by most Timeform adherents,
is that a 137 or higher makes one a truly great racehorse.) Only six countries were represented, as follows:

Britain (England/Ireland) — eighty-one horses

USA — sixty-one

France — forty-one

Australia — six

Italy — four

Japan — one

Spectacular Bid was given a rating of 141 by Morris
and Randall, which put him ninth among all horses on

Earth during the 1900s and third behind Secretariat (second at 144, to Sea-Bird) and Citation (fifth at 142) among the Americans. Seattle Slew, Native Dancer, and Affirmed were the next highest-rated American horses, followed by Man o' War, Alydar, Count Fleet, and Swaps to round out the top ten Americans.

Having proved again that comparisons of horses are ultimately in the eye of the beholder, let it be said that Spectacular Bid met or exceeded every standard by which great racehorses are measured. He was a champion at two, three, and four; set track records sprinting and going long; overcame bad rides and bad judgments; carried weight; repeatedly beat up his contemporaries; and finished his career with a season and a race that would have made him a Hall of Famer even if he had been a prior mediocrity.

He, in fact, came as close as an animal can to validating the tongue-in-cheek bombast of his trainer as "the greatest horse ever to look through a bridle." If not the greatest, he was on the short list of claimants to that title.

*Timothy T. Capps*
*Columbia, Maryland, 2000*

# CHAPTER 1

## *Light On Paper*

**M**ost racehorses that amount to anything, which is to say they win stakes races (something managed by less than three percent of the breed), have pedigrees that on hindsight have a stakes-winning tinge.

The adage that all racehorses are well-bred if one goes back far enough is one of the glorious ironies of a tradition-rich sport. Pedigrees that are to kill for on paper and in the auction ring so often turn out to be road kill on the racetrack.

The archives of statistics now available on Thoroughbreds, past or present, demonstrate that the most certain way of breeding stakes performers is to send stakes-winning and/or -producing mares to proven, top-echelon sires. Done repetitively, this will improve the odds of getting a good horse, but not so absolutely as to eliminate chance or frustrate hopes of the breeder whose stock does not approach such lofty levels.

Occasionally, racing celebrates a horse that is bred to the purple — a Secretariat or Easy Goer — and runs to its pedigree, but most champions make their own registration papers and those of their antecedents improve as a result of their performances.

Spectacular Bid, as was the case with almost all of his nearby great contemporaries, possessed origins that could have made him an also-ran in the pages of Thoroughbred history or the seminal champion he became.

Horses are, of course, the genetic sum of the parts of their pedigrees, and mating decisions are rarely influenced by any careful comparisons of internal aspects of a mare's pedigree with those of potential mates. Mostly, people look at sire lines (who's hot, who's not, what's selling well), at production records of the tail female family, at inbreeding or nicking ideas, and primarily, at affordability.

The mating that resulted in Spectacular Bid was mostly a combination of much of the above, although dashes of happenstance, intuition, and luck also were involved.

His dam, Spectacular, had a California heritage of sorts, being bred and owned by Mrs. William M. Jason and her mother, Mrs. William Gilmore.

The Gilmore family had a lengthy history in Golden State racing, with William S. Gilmore having owned and operated Golden Gate Fields racetrack and the prominent Loma Rica Ranch in central California. When Gilmore died in 1962, a couple of his daughters continued to race a few horses. One daughter, Madelyn Gilmore Jason, partnered with local veterinarian William Linfoot in a To Market mare named Stop On Red, whom they bred to the former handicap standout Promised Land.

Stop On Red herself was one of the breeding game's oddities, a successful twin. Nothing strikes greater fear into the heart of a mare owner or veterinarian than a mare carrying twin follicles. Rarely are twins permitted to see the light of day and rarer still that they race or go on to the breeding shed.

Stop On Red and her sister, Go On Green, bred by the fabled Elmendorf Farm, both raced extensively, were multiple winners, and went on to produce multiple winners, with Stop On Red foaling four stakes runners, including two minor stakes winners.

Her sire, To Market, has a story worth telling because he and his sire, Market Wise, are the only horses to appear twice in the immediate pedigree of Spectacular Bid.

Market Wise was bred by Admiral Cary Grayson in 1938, the year Admiral Grayson, physician to and confidant of Woodrow Wilson, died. A son of Kentucky Derby winner Brokers Tip out of the On Watch mare On Hand, Market Wise was a moderate two-year-old, running without success in claiming races until the distances stretched out.

At three, he was a different animal and a durable one. Starting twenty-six times, he won the Wood Memorial, was third to Whirlaway in the Kentucky Derby, later won the Edgemere, Gallant Fox, and Governor Bowie Handicaps, the Pimlico Special, and the Jockey Club Gold Cup. In the Gold Cup, he had a ding-dong battle with Whirlaway, finally edging the Triple Crown winner by a nose in an American record time of 3:20 4/5 for two miles.

The personification of toughness and consistency, Market Wise contended with the best horses in training and handicappers' weights with distinction. Near the top of the older horse ranks in 1942, when he won the Suburban Handicap, he shared year-end divisional honors in 1943 with Devil Diver and captured the Massachusetts Handicap and Narragansett Special. He started fifty-three times in four years, won $222,140 in an era when six-figure earners were rare, and gained the respect of the country's leading horsemen.

His son To Market was bigger than his sire, more precocious, and not as sound, although he was a major stakes winner who was well regarded enough to spend his stud career at Kentucky's Claiborne Farm, the bluest of blue chips among American stud farms.

To Market, bred and owned by Virginian Sam Mason II, won the Arlington and Washington Park Futurities at two, making him the king of Chicago, but he got bopped by Battlefield in the Futurity at Belmont Park. He was among the best juveniles of 1950 and regarded as a classic prospect in 1951, but was bothered by a variety of injuries as a sophomore and didn't get much done, winning three overnight handicaps in eleven starts.

At four, To Market started in California, winning the San Carlos Handicap, then came East to get his lessons

from Hall of Fame trainer Max Hirsch. He won the Mass 'Cap at one and a quarter miles, the Arlington Handicap, and the Hawthorne Gold Cup. After a three-race stint at five, he was sent to Claiborne to begin a stud career that was solid, if not spectacular. Among his progeny was a filly named High Bid, bred by Gladys Phipps' Wheatley Stable, from the Princequillo mare Stepping Stone.

High Bid won several stakes, the best of them being the prestigious Alabama at Saratoga over one and a quarter miles, but her biggest moment, insofar as this tale goes, came when she foaled a colt in 1962, for the same breeder-owner, who would be named Bold Bidder.

To Market's other daughter of importance in Spectacular Bid's pedigree, the aforementioned Stop On Red, was bred repeatedly to a horse largely forgotten in today's pedigree, but a prominent star of the late 1950s and, for a time, an important carrier of the Teddy sire line in the United States. His name was Promised Land, and he was bred and owned by the Isidor Bieber-Hirsch Jacobs combination that also bred and raced his sire, Palestinian.

Palestinian, a son of Calumet Farm star Sun Again, was a standout for four years, despite running on a bowed tendon much of the time, and was among the best of his division at three and five. Just beaten in the 1949 Preakness by Capot, he won the Jersey Stakes and the Empire City Handicap, and took the Brooklyn and Golden Gate Handicaps at five.

His son Promised Land was a big, gangly gray who earned over a half-million dollars in a lengthy career that encompassed seventy-seven starts. He won twenty-one times, including races like the Pimlico Special and the John B. Campbell and Massachusetts Handicaps.

Promised Land's maternal grandsire, Mahmoud, won the English Derby for the Aga Khan in 1936, then became a leading sire in the United States after being imported by C. V. Whitney. Mahmoud was an interesting cross of speed and stamina, and his progeny reflected both. He was a sire of good grass horses at a time when turf racing on the flat was relatively new in America, and it can be readily supposed that he would have had much greater influence had he come along twenty or thirty years later.

He transmitted to his grandson his gray color and a

fondness for turf (arguably, Promised Land's best race was his win in Santa Anita's one and three-quarters-mile San Juan Capistrano on grass).

The toughness came from Palestinian and his side of the family, and a cross between Promised Land and Stop On Red resulted in a foal whose parents had collectively raced 128 times. The four grandparents, all stakes winners, were as astounding, racing 274 times among them. Finding comparable numbers in today's pedigrees would be unheard of, which tells us something about the changes in American racing and, possibly, the declining constitution of the American Thoroughbred.

The result of the Promised Land—Stop On Red liaison was a gray filly, foaled in 1970 and eventually named Spectacular. Dr. Linfoot was not unduly impressed by her as a yearling and prodded Madelyn Jason to sell the filly at the 1971 Del Mar yearling sale.

Mrs. Jason liked the filly and bid $20,500 for her, buying out Linfoot's share, then sold half-interest in her to her mother, Mrs. Gilmore. Thus, mother and daughter ended up as partners in a filly they raced jointly on the northern California circuit.

Spectacular didn't race until she was three, when she

started ten times, set a track record for six furlongs in 1:09 1/5 at Pleasanton Fair, and was second in the My Fair Lady Stakes at Bay Meadows to a filly named Procne. Fulfilling the "small world" scenario, Procne eventually became the dam of Flying Paster, the classy Cal-bred who was one of Spectacular Bid's main antagonists.

Madelyn Jason had decided to get more active in the commercial breeding business, and while she culled several fillies from her small broodmare operation, she said she had a "feeling" about Spectacular and elected to keep her.

She sent her to Buck Pond Farm near Versailles, Kentucky, which was operated by Mrs. George Proskauer and bloodstock agent Vic Heerman, a Californian who had previously advised the Gilmores.

Mrs. Jason took some heat from California breeders for sending Spectacular to Kentucky, but she had in mind breeding summer sales yearlings and believed that she could best find suitable stallions in Kentucky.

Heerman thought Bold Bidder, a champion son of the brilliant Bold Ruler and sire of 1974 Kentucky Derby winner Cannonade, might match well with Spectacular, so he bought a season to the stallion, who

stood at Gainesway Farm, from prominent owner-breeder John W. Hanes.

If Spectacular was the product of solid bread- and butter-breeding, with a decent but nondescript race record, Bold Bidder was the antithesis. About the only thing he and Spectacular had in common was To Market as maternal grandsire.

Bold Bidder, had he been human, might have grown up neurotic, for much was expected of a horse with his pedigree and connections.

He was bred by the Wheatley Stable of the afore-mentioned Mrs. Phipps, whose purple and gold silks were among the best known in American racing. Her branch of the Phipps family, including son Ogden Phipps (father of Ogden Mills "Dinny" Phipps) and daughter Barbara Janney (mother of Stuart S. Janney III), would race some of the sport's best horses during the post-World War II period.

None of the Phipps horses accomplished more or had a longer lasting influence than Mrs. Phipps' home-bred Bold Ruler, the leading member of the fabulous foal crop of 1954, which also included Gallant Man, Round Table, and Promised Land.

Foaled at Claiborne on the same day as Round Table, Bold Ruler was by the magnificent European-bred and -raced stallion Nasrullah and the rugged Discovery mare Miss Disco.

Nasrullah had a wonderful physique and a horrid temperament, one that probably kept him from being the great racehorse his pedigree suggested he should be. By the unbeaten Nearco out of Mumtaz Begum, a half-sister to the dam of Mahmoud, Nasrullah had superior speed but only an intermittent desire to use it.

Despite his obstinacy, Nasrullah won several valuable races in England, including the Champion Stakes, and was classic-placed. Evaluating his true form was virtually impossible because of his behavioral flaws, but it seems likely he was at his best at distances under one and a half miles, and he possessed excellent acceleration.

Whatever his self-induced racing deficiencies may have cost him, they were of no matter in his stud career. He had the pedigree and looks to be a good stallion, and he exceeded all expectations.

Nasrullah led the English sire list in 1951, the year after an American syndicate purchased him to stand at Claiborne, where he led the North American sire list

five times. He died in 1959 at age nineteen. He sired ninety-nine stakes winners during a time when stallion books were modest compared with those of the late '90s. If he were standing at stud now, he would probably have sired 150-200 stakes winners over a comparable period of years.

The list of champions, classic heroes, and major race winners by Nasrullah is extraordinary and includes Never Say Die, Bald Eagle, Grey Sovereign, Nashua, Red God, Jaipur, Never Bend, and Bold Ruler.

Bold Ruler was possibly his best son on the racetrack and went on to compile a record as a sire that marked him as one of the best stallions of the 20th century. He was born with a hernia the size of a Caribbean country and was plagued throughout his career by various ailments, but he did enough over three seasons against extraordinary competition to be rated nineteenth on *The Blood-Horse*'s top 100 racehorses of the 20th century.

A precocious two-year-old, he won seven of ten races and was thought by many to be the best juvenile in the country, although there were questions about his stamina and soundness.

A free runner with a high cruising speed, he cost himself some races by refusing to rate and fighting restraint, but ended his three-year-old season with Horse of the Year and three-year-old male championship awards after victories in the Preakness, Flamingo Stakes, Jerome Handicap, Vosburgh Stakes, and six other stakes. He carried 130 or more pounds to victory four times.

At four, he was better, although he won no year-end titles. In an abbreviated seven-race campaign, he won five, including the Toboggan, Carter, Stymie, Suburban, and Monmouth Handicaps, and he won under 133 pounds twice, 134 twice, and 135 once. He lost under 135 and 136 pounds.

He had carried his speed to victory over one and a quarter miles three times in excellent company and had won under 130 pounds or more eight times in ten tries.

When he began his stud career at Claiborne in 1959, Bold Ruler had the entire package for success in the American environment: exceptional pedigree, excellent form at two, classic-winning quality, the character and toughness to carry high weights, and both high speed and the ability to carry it through middle distances.

Hopes for him were high, and he exceeded them. His first crop contained only sixteen foals, but eight of them won stakes, and he topped the North American general sire list in 1963, with only two- and three-year-olds on the track.

He led the North American general sire list seven additional times in his career, which lasted until his death at age seventeen, and sired eighty-two stakes winners and eleven champions from 356 named foals. As with his sire, it is tantalizing to consider what he might have done in the era of the eighty-mare (or more) book.

His best offspring was unquestionably the almighty Secretariat, who did everything well, but Bold Ruler was best known for precocious, high-class young horses that had trouble staying healthy. In fact, the knock was that they didn't want to go long, a notion belied by the record books, but people had to find something to complain about.

Interestingly, there was an answer to those who said, and many did, that the Bold Rulers could not carry their speed much beyond a mile in class company. Beginning with Secretariat in 1973, Bold Ruler sons, paternal grandsons, or paternal great-grandsons won six of seven Kentucky Derbys run through 1979, three Preaknesses, three Belmonts, and two Triple Crowns. If his progeny were one dimensional, theirs was a nice dimension to have.

Bold Bidder was a member of Bold Ruler's third crop, foals of 1962, and as luck would have, he was neither a typical son of his sire, nor a very well-regarded one, at least until well into his three-year-old season, after he was sent packing from Wheatley Stable's regal shedrow.

Bold Bidder wasn't awful; he just couldn't match strides with the likes of high-class stablemate Bold Lad, also a member of the '62 class of Bold Rulers, who had great ability but lacked soundness. Bold Bidder, made more like To Market, which is to say leggy and a bit coarse, did not have the early speed of most of his sire's get, and his race record at two demonstrated that whatever merits he possessed as a racehorse might take awhile to surface.

Trainers for high-rent outfits can age in a hurry waiting for well-bred plodders to find themselves. Phipps trainer Eddie Neloy, with Bold Lad, Queen Empress, and a hotshot two-year-old named Buckpasser to tend to, knew when to cut his losses.

Bold Bidder had ankle and attitude problems at two, at which time he went unraced. He wasn't showing Neloy much improvement and was sold to Paul Falkenstein and transferred to trainer Randy Sechrest. Maybe it was the change in stalls, more likely the maturation of a big frame whose body needed time to catch up. Regardless, Bold Bidder started to act like a racehorse by late summer of his three-year-old season and won the Jerome, Hawthorne, Diamond Jubilee, and Ben Franklin Handicaps.

Sent to California for the winter, Bold Bidder, by now leased by John Gaines of Gainesway Farm and his partners, John Hanes and John Olin, continued to progress. He won the Charles H. Strub Stakes in a track record 1:59 3/5 for one and a quarter miles, well in advance of his previous form, and Gaines and company completed his purchase and syndicated him. Sent back East, he stopped in Kentucky to be bred to a few mares before returning to racing.

The new owners parted company with Sechrest during the summer, bringing Woodford C. "Woody" Stephens to the table, and Stephens coaxed three more major stakes wins out of the strapping bay colt.

Bold Bidder won the Monmouth Handicap at one and a quarter miles, the Washington Park Handicap at a mile (running the distance in 1:32 4/5, three-fifths of a second off the then-world record), and the Hawthorne Gold Cup, again at one and a quarter miles, along with the Charles W. Bidwell Memorial Handicap, also at Hawthorne. He was six of fifteen for the year, good enough to be named champion older male in the Thoroughbred Racing Associations' poll of racing secretaries.

Bold Bidder raced once at five, then was retired to Gainesway with a career record of thirty-three starts, thirteen wins, seven placings, $478,021 in earnings, and a championship trophy. He was also remembered as a "different" Bold Ruler, one who, at maturity, had great physical presence, with substantial bone and muscle and great symmetry.

Perhaps not surprisingly, given that his dam was huge and didn't find her best stride until her three-year-old summer, Bold Bidder took time to get his house in order, and he got better with time. There was, in fact, a sense that no one ever quite figured him out, that we never saw the best of him.

His younger half-brother, Top Bid, by high-speed

sire Olympia, also displayed stakes-winning form on the flat, but was not a peak performer until he shifted to steeplechasing, where he improved with age, becoming North America's best jump horse at age six.

Bold Bidder's stud career was solid, if not remarkable. When bred to speed, he tended to get speed; when bred to substance, he tended to get horses that matured later and preferred two-turn races.

He sired the winner of the 100th Kentucky Derby in 1974, Cannonade, and a boatload of good fillies, such as Highest Trump and Cautious Bidder, and was second on the North American sire list in 1974. On balance, his stud career was like that of many sons of Bold Ruler. They did well as sires of runners, but did not become sires of sires, usually leaving behind sons that were solid stallions, but were always capable of getting the occasional standout horse. Those standouts — horses like Ruffian, Seattle Slew, and our hero, Spectacular Bid — were the periodic reminders of the blinding, nearly suffocating brilliance of the Nearco-Nasrullah-Bold Ruler tribe at its finest.

The decision to send Spectacular to a Bold Ruler-line stallion was easy enough, since they were the rage in the mid-1970s, and Vic Heerman's idea was to out-cross her with the premier source of American speed and middle-distance ability and to refine the To Market/Promised Land coarseness. Given that Bold Bidder was an uncharacteristic Bold Ruler, with a good bit of To Market in his make-up, the decision could eas-ily have backfired; instead, the result was nothing short of, well, spectacular.

Bred to Bold Bidder at Gainesway in the spring of 1975, Spectacular foaled an iron-gray colt on February 17, 1976, at Buck Pond. He was partially raised at Buck Pond, but was moved, along with his dam, to Wimbledon Farm in Fayette County, Kentucky, when Heerman's partnership with Mrs. Proskauer ended.

A strongly made yearling, the colt was nominated to the Keeneland July sale, the Tiffany's of yearling auc-tions, then and now, but was rejected when the Keeneland selection committee determined that his female family was too weak. In hindsight, this was a questionable call, but at the time the black type in the family, while readily available, was modest. One had to go back to the sixth dam, whose half-sister produced 1929 two-year-old champion Whichone, rival of

Gallant Fox, to find anything important. That does not get a horse into Keeneland July, so he went into the September version instead.

According to Heerman, a number of lookers stopped by to see the colt at Keeneland, and he and Mrs. Jason thought he would fetch $60,000 or so. Setting no reserve because she wanted to be assured of a sale, Mrs. Jason watched the hammer fall at $37,000, the winning bidders being the Maryland-based Hawksworth Farm of Harry C. Meyerhoff; his wife, Teresa; and son, Tom Meyerhoff.

Harry Meyerhoff, an industrial engineer by education, had joined his family's construction business in Baltimore after college and worked with his brother Bob to expand into real-estate development and management. Both were racing fans for years before they made their first foray into ownership in 1963 with a couple of claiming horses.

They started buying moderately priced yearlings at the Keeneland fall sale in 1965, racing them under the name Bon Etage Farm. They liked the Bold Ruler line, as did most people at the time, and their best horse was a 1971 Keeneland purchase by the Bold Ruler stallion

Disciplinarian. Named Ecole Etage, he won a couple of stakes, earned $241,525, and actually led Secretariat into the first turn of the 1973 Preakness, when that particular son of Bold Ruler decided to get on with business.

Harry Meyerhoff retired from the company in 1973 because he was "tired of working" and didn't have to anymore. Two years later, the brothers' racing partnership ended. Harry Meyerhoff started racing on his own, although he followed the same modus operandi and bought yearlings at Keeneland in September, giving them to Maryland trainer Grover G. "Bud" Delp to train.

An earlier purchase of a Bold Bidder filly, named Bold Place, a stakes winner of more than $100,000, resold in foal to Riva Ridge for $250,000, left Meyerhoff with a soft spot for Bold Bidder, so it was entirely logical for the Meyerhoffs and Delp to inspect the son of Spectacular.

The Hawksworth team concentrated on the Keeneland fall sale because of what Tom Meyerhoff described as "a matter of economics." They felt that as many good racehorses came out of the fall sale as from July, and since residual value, meaning an expensive pedigree, did not mean much to them, September was their shopping place.

The Meyerhoffs would review the catalog, looking at every page, choose the ones they wanted to see based on the pedigree, then turn the conformation part over to Delp.

In 1977, the gray Bold Bidder—Spectacular colt was the one they chose to focus on, and Delp saw a tightly muscled athletic fellow he liked instantly, enough so that the Meyerhoffs were prepared to go to $50,000 or more to get him, above their usual purchase limit.

Harry Meyerhoff recalls: "We thought we might have to pay more than we did, but he had a twin in his dam's family, and Bold Bidder was not particularly popular as a sire. He was a standout physically, a very well-conformed yearling who toed out a little in his right front. That might have affected his price a little."

Thus, the $37,000 number, disappointing to Mrs. Jason and her mother, was pleasing to the purchasers, who sent their new acquisition, and others, to the Middleburg, Virginia, training center where he was broken and taught the early lessons of a racehorse by veteran horsewoman Barbara Graham.

The adventures that awaited them and the gray colt were beyond even the vivid imagination of Bud Delp.

# CHAPTER 2

## *"...He can really run."*

M aryland's racing roots run deep, dating back to the early 1700s, and only New York can rival it for longevity and quality of tradition.

Maryland's love affair with horses began on the flat, sandy soil of its eastern shore, which is still a haven for agriculture. Near the Chesapeake Bay or along the rivers of southern Maryland, holders of English land grants raised cattle, tobacco, corn, and horses, racing the latter at local fairs. If the horses were good enough, they raced at the Annapolis track operated by the Maryland Jockey Club, chartered in 1743 and now the parent company of Laurel and Pimlico.

If Maryland's early settlers were culturally diverse, they shared their interest in horses. Breeding and racing were soon commonplace throughout the state. Central Maryland, home to Baltimore, became the most populous area of the state, and Baltimore County, a large area surrounding the city and stretching to Pennsylvania, is today regarded as the heartland of the Maryland horse community.

Say that, though, to a Marylander and you'll get at least a debate, if not an argument.

They'll remind you that Northern Dancer gained his international reputation as a stallion in Cecil County, that several of the state's best-known stud farms are in neighboring Harford County, that fox-hunting and chasing, long-time staples of the Maryland horse culture, are still prevalent in Howard and Montgomery counties, etc.

If they know some history, they'll tell you about Sam Riddle's farm near the ocean in Berlin, Maryland, where Man o' War and most of his illustrious offspring got their first racing lessons or about America's first great breeding farm, Belair Stud, in Bowie, where famed colonial mare Selima first grazed, and two centuries later, equine legends Gallant Fox, Omaha, and Nashua first stretched their legs.

You will hear the stories about Alfred Vanderbilt's Sagamore Farm and his choice to retire the mighty Native Dancer to stud in Maryland instead of Kentucky.

William Woodward Sr., breeder-owner of Gallant Fox, Omaha, and Nashua, believed the air off the Chesapeake was good for young horses, a notion still widely accepted in Maryland. Pride in tradition and an innate belief that He, the Almighty, put horses and Maryland together for a reason have sustained an industry through almost three centuries of dealing with the slings and arrows of outrageous fortune.

The state had year-round racing before any jurisdiction outside the Sun Belt. This was convenient for local horsemen, who could venture elsewhere when it suited them, meaning when they had a horse capable of shipping out of town to steal one, whether it be a claimer in Delaware or a major stakes in New York.

Canny and thrifty by nature, Maryland horsemen have always placed a premium on value, preferring soundness and consistency to market fashion and hype. The late John Finney, long-time president of Fasig-Tipton Sales Company, once called Maryland "the home of the hundred-cent dollar," a grudging salute to the horsemen of the Free State and their sense of stewardship.

Glamour wasn't their game, but they knew how to live within their means, and Maryland acquired a rep-

utation over the years as a place where out-of-towners had best bring a runner with them, especially in the claiming and allowance ranks.

With year-round racing and that value-driven culture, Maryland evolved into the prototype claiming circuit. Shrewd trainers became specialists in combing the claiming ranks with a skill and ferocity unmatched anywhere, and most of Maryland's best-known horsemen cut their teeth — some say grew their teeth — on the claiming game.

Grover G. Delp (he was called Bud from early childhood on) was born in farm country — cattle, horses, forage crops — in Harford County, Maryland, in 1933. He was around racehorses pretty early in life, going to the races as a youngster at nearby Havre de Grace and Bel Air racetracks, and at Pimlico, Laurel, Bowie, Timonium, and the state's various fair tracks.

Delp's father was drowned in an accident when his son was eighteen months old, and Delp's mother remarried when he was nine.

Her new husband was Raymond B. Archer, who had been training horses in Maryland since about the time of Man o' War. He was known as a thorough horseman and a self-made one, having started training his first racehorse at age twenty-five. Young Delp, bitten by the racing bug early, started going to work in the mornings with his stepfather during his early teens.

Archer, unsentimental about the game, didn't encourage Delp. In fact, he tried to discourage him with reminders of how difficult the lifestyle of a horse trainer can be. But Delp, who liked the simple dedication to horses of the grooms and hotwalkers, the quiet of the post-workout periods, and the action in the afternoons, was insistent on living life as a racetracker.

He worked for Archer as a hotwalker, a pony boy, and a groom until, goaded by his mother, he enrolled at the University of Maryland. Delp said he had cut classes in high school to get to the track, and unfortunately for his scholarly future, the pattern continued at College Park.

Eventually, his insistence on being a student of racing caused university officials to decide that he should spend his time someplace other than college. However, his road to the racetrack was detoured when Uncle Sam beckoned Delp on to the U.S. Army.

After his Army tour, he returned home to work for his stepfather as assistant trainer, a spot he occupied for about six years and might have for longer had Archer's parsimony not gotten in the way.

Delp, being paid $125 a week with a wife and baby and another on the way, asked for a raise, telling Archer that if he didn't get one he would go out on his own. Archer didn't respond, so after a week Delp gave his notice and launched his first independent operation.

Bud Delp, country-boy smart and breezily confident, took to his home state's highly competitive claiming world like tourists do to Maryland crab cakes, soon elevating himself to the top ranks among local conditioners. He was running a fast-paced thirty-two-horse outfit that had him at the top of Laurel's trainer list. Then, on November 3, 1964, Delp was visited by the ultimate horseman's horror — a stable fire at Laurel Park that wiped out all but two of his string.

Devastated, he nonetheless plunged back in via the claims box and was soon rolling again, winning the trainer's title at the next Pimlico race meeting.

Delp's skill with cheap horses did not go unnoticed. He eventually got a shot at training some horses for E. P. Taylor's Windfields Farm and for the partnership of Harry Meyerhoff and Robert Meyerhoff.

While claiming was his main focus (he averaged more than 200 wins a year for the five years prior to Spectacular Bid's arrival), Delp had some notable stakes winners over the next ten years, including Kentucky Oaks winner Sweet Alliance, Dancing Champ, What a Summer, Leader of the Band, Pro Bidder, Bold Place, Hay Patcher, Ecole Etage, and Shenandoah River.

Some of those horses were yearling sale purchases, including a few relatively expensive ones such as Sweet Alliance ($65,000) and Hay Patcher ($70,000), demonstrating that Delp could shop at Tiffany's as well as Kmart. Still, he had not had a shot at a big hitter, the kind usually bought on hot summer nights at Keeneland or Saratoga for six figures or more by people intoxicated by the moment as much as by the horse they are buying.

Thus the lean but strong gray son of Bold Bidder that Delp liked enough to tell Harry Meyerhoff he ought to go upward of $50,000 to get seemed to be another cookie-cutter Delp yearling buy.

He seemed out of the ordinary, though, to Barbara Graham, who thought he was "the best-looking yearling" she'd ever seen, and while learning his early lessons under her watchful eye at the Middleburg training center, he demonstrated the will and common sense one looks for in good horses.

Delp's record during the years prior to Bid's arrival under his shedrow was one of remarkable accomplishment, even without the superstar horse or two to light the path. He actually won more races in 1965 (ninety-seven) than he had in 1964 (ninety) prior to the disastrous barn fire.

After that, he went from strength to strength, topping the century mark in wins for the first time in 1967 with 111, which placed him sixth among North American trainers. From '67 through '77, the year before Spectacular Bid's juvenile season, he was among the top ten North American trainers in races won, winning more than 200 races four of those years, including 239 during Bid's two-year-old year.

The upgrades in the quality of his stock pushed his stable's earnings steadily north, climbing above $1 million for the first time in 1975 and placing him in the top ten in trainer earnings nationally on a regular basis thereafter.

Delp loved the action of the claiming game, and he was one of the best players around, but he yearned for the opportunity that had come the way of Billy Turner (Seattle Slew) and Laz Barrera (Affirmed) — to go to the hunt with an elephant gun.

Delp brought the gray colt, named by now Spectacular Bid, to Pimlico in early spring and soon saw the eagerness and speed in morning trials he'd hoped for.

Harry Meyerhoff says that it was another member of the Delp clan, son Gerald, who first touted the colt to his owners. "We had a stakes winner named Tiger Castle who was our star, and we were looking at him one day when Gerald said, 'You'd better pay attention to this gray; he can really run.' "

Riding him some in the morning and, eventually, in the afternoon was a local kid named Ronnie Franklin, an apprentice jockey with a brashness that Delp could identify with, but also knew he needed to control.

The Spectacular Bid-Franklin duo debuted at Pimlico in a maiden special weight going five and a half furlongs on June 30, 1978. The adventures in front of the two could hardly have been forecast, but the Hawksworth Farm color bearer went off at 6-1, the crowd's fourth choice behind William Farish's well-bred Hoist the Flag colt Strike Your Colors (4-1), who was making his second start. Instant Love was the favorite at 7-5, followed by Cinder Luck at 7-2.

Franklin sent Bid to the front as soon as the gate doors opened, and he wired his field, as the saying goes, coming home three and a quarter lengths in front of the Hoist the Flag colt in the running time of 1:04 3/5, only two-fifths of a second off Old Hilltop's track record.

Splashy debuts are often a prescription for future disappointment, and Bid's second start on July 22 at Pimlico would be carefully watched.

The fans were more certain, betting him down to 3-10. He and Franklin were teamed up again, but this time with a different script. Third in the early going, he pushed past the leaders going into the turn, steadily increased his margin, then drew away "with authority," in chart-caller vernacular, to win by eight lengths. His time for the five and a half-furlong event was 1:04 1/5, equaling the track record and suggesting his readiness for bigger things.

Eleven days later he was at Monmouth Park on the Jersey shore for the Tyro Stakes, a traditional early East Coast two-year-old stakes. The trip could not have gone worse.

The Tyro was split into two divisions, and heavy rains left the racetrack sloppy, a condition that usually favors speed. For the first time, Bid showed none of that, breaking last and trailing the field early while racing wide. Favored at 8-5, he could only pass tiring horses to finish a disconcerting fourth to winner Groton High.

Delp had, according to Harry Meyerhoff, told Franklin to let the colt "play" in the slop at Monmouth and believed that the conditions led to his defeat, so he sent him back out eighteen days later in the Dover Stakes at Delaware Park.

Delaware fans, forgiving his muddy track failure, made him even-money favorite in the Dover, where he again faced Strike Your Colors. As at Monmouth, he got away slowly and was blocked coming around the final turn, when Franklin chose not to go for a narrow opening at the half-mile pole.

Strike Your Colors had gotten loose on the lead turning for home and Spectacular Bid could not catch him, finishing second by two and a half lengths, the winner going six furlongs in 1:10 4/5 on a fast surface.

Heading into the fall campaign, the best that could be said about the gray son of Bold Bidder and Spectacular

was that he had some talent, but more promise than achievement thus far. He was zero for two in stakes company and had not yet been asked to face his division's toughest challenges.

Delp chose Atlantic City Race Course's World's Playground Stakes, then a valuable and meaningful juvenile testing ground, for Bid's next outing, and what America saw was a revelation.

Facing six others, including Belmont Futurity winner Crest of the Wave, a Crozier colt owned by Fred Hooper, Groton High, and, of course, Strike Your Colors, Bid would make his 5-1 starting odds seem like a monumental misjudgment.

Racing over a "good" track, Franklin hustled Bid out of the gate and split horses to take the lead after an opening quarter-mile in :22.

He was two lengths ahead after a half-mile in :44 3/5 and six lengths up at the eighth pole in 1:09 for six furlongs. Taking no prisoners, he ripped off a final furlong in :11 4/5, stopping the teletimer in 1:20 4/5 for seven furlongs, two-fifths of a second off the Atlantic City record for the distance.

One could give a glib racing surface at least partial

credit for the flashy fractions, but his fifteen-length margin of victory over second-place Crest of the Wave was Secretariat-like.

Now the world was watching.

In those pre-Breeders' Cup days, two-year-old championships were rarely won without a significant victory in New York, so Delp put the prestigious Champagne Stakes at Belmont Park, run two weeks after the World's Playground, on Bid's agenda.

This was a serious step, and Delp chose to change riders, going to Jorge Velasquez, one of the country's leading big-race pilots and regular rider of Alydar, who had thrilled the nation with his dramatic efforts against Triple Crown winner Affirmed.

The ante also was raised on the racetrack, for Bid would be going up against Bert and Diana Firestone's General Assembly, a good-looking member of Secretariat's second crop and winner of Saratoga's Hopeful Stakes; Calumet Farm's unbeaten Nashua colt Tim the Tiger, winner of the Sapling and Cowdin Stakes; and Crest of the Wave.

A fifteen-length win over well-regarded youngsters notwithstanding, Bid would go off at 5-2 in the one-

mile Champagne, behind General Assembly at 7-5 and Tim the Tiger at 17-10.

Coming away from the inside post position in a six-horse field, Bid broke moderately, but had the leader, Harbor View Farm's Breezing On, collared after an opening quarter in :23 1/5.

Staying well off the rail, he took the field through a half in :46, then opened up by four lengths through the stretch, with General Assembly, Tim the Tiger, and Crest of the Wave in vain pursuit.

In comfortable command, Velasquez brought him home by two and three-quarters lengths over General Assembly in 1:34 4/5 for the mile, a time equaled or bettered in the Champagne only by champion Count Fleet (1:34 4/5 in 1942), champion Vitriolic (1:34 3/5 in 1967), and champion Seattle Slew (1:34 2/5 in 1976). Slew's dazzler left many watchers feeling they had seen the next Triple Crown winner, and they had. Bid's performance started similar talk. Harry Meyerhoff remembers the Champagne as an especially "...big thrill. It was great to see him beat the New York horses and just breeze in doing so."

Delp, not one to miss opportunity's knocks, decided to keep the colt racing in metropolitan New York, sending him to the Meadowlands in New Jersey only eleven days after the Champagne for the rich one and one-sixteenth-mile Young America Stakes.

There were some who questioned bringing him back so quickly after back-to-back power performances, and possibly they were right.

Running under the lights for the first time, but seemingly facing lesser opponents, Bid was 3-10 in the Young America and gave his heavy backers a test of their cardiovascular systems.

Getting sandwiched at the start by, among others, Strike Your Colors, Bid lost several lengths, but Velasquez rushed him up to a position just off the leader.

The pair went for the lead in the early stretch and got it, with expectations that they would put their early troubles behind and draw away comfortably.

Uneasy rumbles were heard when Strike Your Colors, fresh from a victory in Keeneland's Breeders' Futurity and in receipt of three pounds, surged on the outside to take a head lead with only an eighth of a mile to go. He was then joined by Pen-Y-Bryn Farm's Instrument Landing, who carried nine fewer pounds than Bid.

After redeeming himself so resoundingly, was he about to be beaten by an earlier nemesis? Urged on by a concerned Velasquez, he found enough to edge away from Strike Your Colors, winning by a neck with Instrument Landing only a head away in third. His time of 1:43 1/5 was a second over the track record on a night when the Hawksworth colt was perhaps not on his game.

With a solid leg up on the season's two-year-old championship, Spectacular Bid nonetheless still had a chance to lose it. Delp, not pleased with Velasquez' work in the Young America, restored Franklin to the irons for the colt's next outing, back on home grounds, in the Laurel Futurity, nine days after the Young America. Yes, Franklin would be back in the saddle, said Delp, but he was kinda hoping to get Bill Shoemaker on his horse in the future. Shoemaker was not available for the Futurity, but Delp made sure the "Shoe" knew he could have Bid's reins whenever he wanted. "He's the best there is," said Delp, "and we want the very best for this colt."

That included racetracks, and both Delp and LeRoy Jolley, trainer of General Assembly, who also was pointing toward the race, were highly critical of the Laurel strip a few days before the Futurity.

Both blamed inordinately slow times in the Laurel fall meet's early races on a deep, shoe-sucking, cuppy track, and Delp said his horse would stay in the barn unless improvements were made.

The track was tended to, and Bid's :47 1/5 half-mile work on Wednesday before the Futurity more than satisfied Delp as to the condition of the horse and the track.

Facing only General Assembly, Tim the Tiger, and Will Farish's multiple stakes winner Clever Trick, Bid figured to be prominent from the outset. The one and one-sixteenth mile Futurity was run out of Laurel's old mile chute and completed at a second finish line a sixteenth of a mile beyond the regular wire.

Delp, worried that an anxious Franklin might forget the finish-line change, had him work three horses on the morning of the race to the second wire.

Franklin, having that part down pat, was more concerned about making sure the colt didn't relax too much once he was on the lead.

Delp instructed him to go to the front, keep the horse relaxed, then, when they turned for home,

"show folks how much horse you have." Franklin sent Bid straight to the lead over Clever Trick, getting the quarter in :23 4/5, a canter for him, the half in :46 4/5, and a two-length lead.

Moving onto the far turn, Clever Trick was done, but Steve Cauthen was asking General Assembly for some run and getting a response.

The splashy chestnut edged up to Bid at the three-sixteenths pole, narrowing his lead to a head, and here was the moment everyone was waiting for, the race for the two-year-old male Eclipse Award.

Actually, what the Laurel crowd saw was more of a triumphal procession than a dramatic duel in the sun.

Franklin loosened the reins and pushed Bid with his hands. The response was quick and gratifying. Widening with every stride, Bid roared past the six-teenth pole in 1:35 1/5 and under the second wire in front of local racing skeptics — Franklin remembered — in 1:41 3/5, a new track record.

The coal-colored colt had, after running six furlongs in 1:11, thrown in a :24 1/5 fourth quarter to run General Assembly into the ground, the way 4-5 favorites are supposed to do. The latter was eight and a half lengths back in second, with Clever Trick twelve lengths away in third.

This was, clearly, the performance of the year among two-year-olds, and it set the seal on his championship honors. An elated Delp kissed Franklin on the cheek when he dismounted, then surprised visiting writers by announcing that Bid was not done for the year.

"If he comes out of this race all right, he'll finish the year in the Heritage at Keystone (now Philadelphia Park)," Delp said.

What Spectacular Bid had left to prove as a juvenile was a puzzle to many, but Delp, loving every minute in the spotlight with the first horse of this caliber he had trained, was envisioning a traveling road show.

Six horses, none bearing the reputations of his earlier autumnal foes, were sent out to face him in the one and one-sixteenth-mile Heritage on Armistice Day, November 11.

The Philly crowd sent the colt off at 1-10, and many must have gulped hard as they saw Bid break slowly, then settle back in fifth place traveling down the backstretch.

Was this a signal the colt had run one too many

times this year? Could he possibly have his colors low-ered by a bunch of allowance horses?

Franklin kept Bid behind and to the outside of the leaders into and around the final turn, asking his horse to run about midway through the bend and having him make up five lengths in less than a furlong.

Keeping the pressure on, Franklin smacked Bid sev-eral times in the early stretch, then hand rode as they drew away to a six-length victory in 1:42.

Turned out Delp had decided to use the Heritage as a training camp, trying to get Spectacular Bid to wait behind other horses, rate off the pace, then go get his horses when asked.

That he did so in impeccable fashion was pleasing to Delp, who said that, yes, after four races in thirty-four days, Bid would go home to Laurel and rest.

In fact, he said, he planned to work him while keep-ing him with his other seventy horses in training until year-end, when he would head for Gulfstream Park. Delp said he had asked for only one stall at Gulfstream — "that's all I need."

Most trainers of classic hopefuls are publicly cau-tious, i.e., "We'll take it one race at a time."

Not Delp, who had his campaign planned: a prep for the Florida Derby, then the Florida Derby, Hialeah's Flamingo Stakes, the Blue Grass Stakes at Keeneland, and the Kentucky Derby.

Still, Delp captured the spirit of the moment when, after the Heritage Stakes, he said of the Kentucky Derby, "It will be the first Derby for all of us, the Meyerhoffs and me, and all because of the kind of horse you dream of." Was this to be wishful thinking, or more Delp hyperbole, or would Spectacular Bid be "the kind of horse you dream of"?

With seven wins in nine starts, two new track records, a track-record equaling performance, and $384,484 in earnings, Spectacular Bid had his championship and winter-book favoritism for the Kentucky Derby and Triple Crown.

There was, however, some noise in the West over something called Flying Paster, a colt named after a type of printing equipment, who was bred and owned by B. J. Ridder of the Knight-Ridder newspaper chain.

Upon closer examination, it was found that Flying Paster was a son of none other than Procne, who beat

the Bid's dam, Spectacular, in a minor stakes at Bay Meadows when they were juveniles.

Ridder had bred her to the Fleet Nasrullah stallion Gummo, a solid California-based sire, and their son, like his eastern counterpart, came to the races with high hopes attached.

His early races, though promising, were not as spectacular as Bid's. Flying Paster won his debut easily, then finished second in three consecutive stakes.

But the tide turned and he ripped off six consecutive victories, all in stakes company, all in California.

He won the De Anza Stakes at Del Mar (six furlongs in 1:08 4/5), the Balboa Stakes at the same track (a mile in 1:35 3/5), the Del Mar Futurity (a mile in 1:34 4/5), the Sunny Slope Stakes at the Oak Tree meet at Santa Anita (seven furlongs in 1:22), the Norfolk Stakes at Oak Tree (one and one-sixteenth miles in 1:42 1/5), and the California Breeders Championship at Santa Anita (seven furlongs in 1:21 4/5).

Flying Paster had won seven of ten starts and earned $376,860. His fast race times could be partially attributed to glib western surfaces, but the consistency of those times and his tractable racing style made him a formidable threat for the Triple Crown races, and West Coast analysts thought he ranked with the best juveniles seen in those parts since the days of Swaps. He appeared to be a genuine two-turn horse, and New York racing secretary Tommy Trotter would place him at 123 pounds on the Experimental Free Handicap, only three pounds below Spectacular Bid.

Reservations about Spectacular Bid's rating were reflected in his Experimental weighting. The Experimental was first published in 1933 by The Jockey Club as a theoretical rating, using weights, of the previous season's leading two-year-olds. The publishers were always careful to say that the Experimental was simply an evaluation of horses based on their juvenile form, and nothing more should be read into it than that. This pronouncement was, of course, widely ignored by racing buffs, who used the Experimental as fodder for winter-time debates over the merits of Triple Crown prospects. (There were two races in the spring in New York cleverly called the Experimental Free Handicap, Nos. 1 and 2, run at six furlongs and one and one-sixteenth miles, respectively, for horses weighted on the Experimental. They

were preps for the Wood Memorial, but died for lack of entries in the late '50s.)

Top weight for colts and geldings on the Experimental is 126, scale weight for three-year-olds at the classic distances. Since the Experimental's origins, only fifteen horses have ever been assigned more than 126, with Count Fleet's 132 the all-time topper. Bimelech (1939), Native Dancer (1952), Bold Lad (1964), and Arazi (1991) were all pegged at 130.

Thus, Spectacular Bid's 126, while scarcely an embarrassment since animals the caliber of Whirlaway, Citation, Tom Fool, Buckpasser, Seattle Slew, and Affirmed received the same number, was testament to the notion that Trotter, and many veteran horsemen, thought Bid had challenges to meet on the road to greatness.

His trainer, at least, was ready.

# CHAPTER 3

## *On The Brink Of Greatness*

T he decade of the '70s was, arguably, the golden age of American racing.

Twenty-five years of frustration ended with Secretariat's epochal thirty-one-length victory in the 1973 Belmont Stakes, which completed his sweep of the Triple Crown. So many notable horses had tried and failed in the Triple Crown series since Citation's "Triple" in 1948 that industry pundits questioned whether a single horse would again capture all three races.

Their pessimistic rationale held that modern Thoroughbreds were more fragile, more speed oriented, and possessed less stamina than their predecessors of earlier times; the standard "things were better in the good old days" canard. Largely ignored was the more meaningful fact that foal crops more than quadrupled in size from Citation's (5,819) to Secretariat's (24,954), greatly expanding the scope of the competitive pool. It would take a supremely talented, versatile, and robust horse to win the Kentucky Derby, Preakness, and Belmont, and Secretariat was all those things and more.

The marvelously sculptured son of Bold Ruler so captured imaginations that he was almost mystical by the time he retired. He was such a statistical phenomenon that, like the horse with whom he was most often compared, Man o' War, it was thought his equal would not be seen again.

If this was so, it was only by a matter of degree, for Secretariat's cropmate, the hulking gelding Forego, carved out a dominating presence in the handicap division during the mid-1970s. Forego, racing through six seasons, captured eight year-end championships, including three Horse of the Year awards. Despite being burdened by massive weights and plagued by persistent leg problems, Forego won twenty-four stakes and earned more than $1.9 million.

A contemporary of Forego's, for an all too brief period, was the magical filly Ruffian, whose startling beauty and fiery spirit captured widespread public interest before her unbeaten record and, ultimately her life, ended when a shattered ankle stopped her effort in a match race with 1975 Derby winner Foolish Pleasure.

In 1977, a burly grandson of Bold Ruler named Seattle Slew, a peerless front runner, became the first horse to win the Triple Crown while still unbeaten in his career. He went on to a record fourteen wins in seventeen starts and would leave the racetrack with a reputation for towering speed and indomitable courage.

In 1978, two chestnuts, one a son of Raise a Native and the other a grandson of that superb sire, would lead a good crop of three-year-olds into the classics. The former, named Alydar and owned by the storied Calumet Farm, flashed superior form in all three Triple Crown races, but became the first horse to finish second in each of the races. He finished behind Raise a Native's grandson Affirmed, who became North America's eleventh Triple Crown winner and the third one in the '70s.

Spectacular Bid had completed a two-year-old season that was on par with the megastars, but could he, his flamboyant trainer, and cocksure young jockey keep the '70s torch burning?

The answer would begin to emerge in Florida, where Delp and his one-stall stable drew constant attention at

Gulfstream Park as Bid got ready for his debut in the seven-furlong Hutcheson Stakes on February 7.

Delp had the tautly muscled gray colt breezing in late December, then started to turn the crank around the third week of January.

The colt worked six furlongs in 1:12 on January 20; seven days later he breezed the same distance in 1:13. His trainer, feeling he needed a race-like outing to be sharp for the Hutcheson, then sent him six and a half furlongs from the starting gate only three days after the January 27 breeze. His move made headlines in the next day's *Daily Racing Form*.

He ripped off the six and a half in 1:15 2/5, only two-fifths off the track record, and galloped out seven furlongs in 1:22 4/5, a second off the Gulfstream mark.

The workout left a lot of veteran horsemen shaking their heads in amazement, including several with designs on the Hutcheson. The result: a four-horse field; just what Delp wanted.

Bid's opposition included the very fast Northern Prospect, a Mr. Prospector colt trained by Jimmy Croll, multiple stakes winner Lot o' Gold, and Canadian juvenile champion Medaille d'Or.

The track, expecting Bid's heavy favoritism to create a minus show pool (insufficient funds to pay those with winning show tickets), permitted win and exacta wagering only. Despite the small field and wagering restrictions, a record Wednesday afternoon crowd of 17,374 showed up to see Bid and Ronnie Franklin, himself an Eclipse Award winner as the nation's leading apprentice jockey, make their 1979 debut as 1-20 favorites.

Northern Prospect bounced away from the gate in front, with Bid lapped on him and Lot o' Gold close behind.

They remained that way into the far turn, through the quarter in :22 4/5 and a half in :44 4/5. On the final turn, just past the three-eighths pole, Northern Prospect edged away from Bid, opening up a one and a half-length lead to the consternation of the crowd.

Intermittent rain during the day had left the track a bit cuppy, and Franklin said afterward that his horse was having trouble at that point finding the track's bottom. Franklin tightened the reins, eased him back, then touched Bid on the shoulder with his whip.

The gray colt immediately slipped inside Northern Prospect and was soon alone in the homestretch. He won easily by three and three-quarters lengths over Lot o' Gold, with Northern Prospect another seven and a half lengths behind. Spectacular Bid traveled six furlongs in 1:08 4/5, seven in 1:21 2/5, a track record. He gave eight pounds to his two closest competitors.

Delp was his normal subdued self afterward, wondering where a field could be found to face his horse in the Fountain of Youth Stakes on February 19.

Smiley Adams, trainer of the runner-up, showed even less caution, saying Lot o' Gold would not only run in the Fountain of Youth, but that he would beat Bid.

Whatever Adams thought he saw was not seen by others, and Lot o' Gold was one of only five to line up against Bid in the Fountain of Youth, among them Tropical Park Derby winner Bishop's Choice and the well-liked Calumet Farm gelding Rivalero.

Bid didn't break with alacrity, and Franklin found himself in a box behind early leader Bishop's Choice and Rivalero. Rivalero moved to the lead going into the backstretch, and Franklin took his horse to the outside. At that point, the stewards could have made the result official, for Spectacular Bid had the race to himself.

He went to the front at about the five-eighths pole

under restraint, then settled on the lead and waited for challengers. Rivalero tried to stay with him and couldn't. Lot o' Gold made a run entering the stretch that took him into second place, but Bid, with occasional reminders from his rider, strolled away to an eight-and-a-half-length victory in 1:41 1/5, a second off the track record.

This time, the track allowed win and place betting, a financial miscue that resulted in a $20,602 minus place pool, so both Bid's opponents and the track took a bath.

A few days later, Delp acknowledged that the Meyerhoffs had insured Bid for $10 million, an unusual act that underscored the potential value of the horse to both his owners and to prospective stallion marketers and breeders.

On March 6, Gulfstream staged its most prestigious race, the Florida Derby, then and now one of the serious prep races for the Kentucky Derby. It was the twenty-eighth running of the event, and few Florida Derbys would be as well-remembered for what could have happened. Bid was 1-20 against six other rivals, including Lot o' Gold, but his main adversary would turn out to be his jockey.

The colt bounced off the left side of the starting gate at the break, then almost ran up the backside of Sir Ivor Again midway through the first turn and had to be checked, losing several lengths.

Franklin, with the proverbial ton of horse underneath him, panicked and rushed Bid up the crowded inside going into the final turn, encountered immovable traffic and had to check again. He then dropped back and swung his horse four wide turning into the stretch, whacked him six times as they straightened away for the stretch run, then finally got clear to draw away by four and a half lengths in a final time of 1:48 4/5 for one and one-eighth miles.

Bid was now three-for-three, but Franklin's future as his pilot was in doubt. The youngster, a local kid from Baltimore who showed up at the stable gate looking for a job and was hired by Delp, owed his brief career to Delp and his sons, with whom he lived.

Observers recalled that Delp had replaced him with Jorge Velasquez the previous fall, but had gone back to Franklin after the Young America Stakes when Velasquez didn't please the trainer. He had spoken then of wanting to get Bill Shoemaker, and the Shoe's name came up again after the Florida Derby, as did some less-than-complimentary remarks by Delp about his house guest.

He was visibly tongue-lashing the rider after the race and continued to do so in front of the media with Franklin standing by, embarrassed.

Delp said he might replace Franklin although he felt the colt ran well for him. He also said, "Ronnie didn't know what he was doing out there. You couldn't make that many mistakes against a horse like Flying Paster and get away with it. I don't want Spectacular Bid ever to lose again."

Unable to keep it at that, Delp said Shoemaker, Darrel McHargue, and Jacinto Vasquez were on his short list of potential jockeys for his ace, but pointedly noted that neither Angel Cordero Jr. nor Velasquez would ever ride him, supposedly for their tactics aboard other horses in the Florida Derby.

Bid had one more Florida engagement on his calendar, the venerable Flamingo Stakes at Hialeah, Florida's oldest Triple Crown prep at the state's most storied track.

The main drama around the fiftieth Flamingo was whether Delp would ask his feed man to ride his horse, because Hialeah's best efforts could produce nothing more than seven allowance horses to face Bid, all of them clearly running for the minor placings or hoping that Bid would forget why he was out there.

After all of Delp's bombast following the Florida Derby, it was Ron Franklin who showed up in the Hialeah paddock wearing the Hawksworth Farm silks prior to the Flamingo. He looked like an attachment to Delp's right arm as the two talked before he mounted Bid.

The pair broke quickly this time, stayed close to pace-setting Gallant Serenade, slid by him coming out of the first turn, and loped along with a one-length lead going into the final turn.

Delp had told his rider that "if he's getting hold of the track all right, let him strut. He loves it."

Maybe Delp was talking more about himself with the strutting stuff, but no matter. Franklin loosened the reins, and Bid put on a show, rolling through six furlongs in 1:09 3/5 and opening up a ten-length lead. He got a few taps from Franklin in the stretch to keep him focused and won by a recorded twelve lengths, although the margin appeared greater. The final time was 1:48 2/5.

A few people wondered why the horse was asked to open up that much when more testing challenges lay just ahead, but more took the approach of *The Blood-Horse* editor Kent Hollingsworth, who wrote after the Flamingo:

"Concern over the level of quality in recent crops is idle, for it is unascertainable. Opinion as to greatness of an individual horse, drawn by comparison to memories of greatness in earlier champions, has no weight.

"The fact is Spectacular Bid is far superior to any of his contemporaries. He does not just beat them; he runs off from them with contemptuous ease. He is a real good horse. It is a waste of time trying to find an excuse not to sit back and enjoy him."

Delp would keep Bid in Florida until April 8, when he was shipped to Keeneland for the upcoming Blue Grass Stakes on April 26. Bid jogged or galloped regularly, breezed on April 13, then was sent out for a seven-furlong stiffener on April 17 between races.

To say he was impressive would be to cheapen the impression he made. Bid took only 1:22 3/5 to get the seven furlongs, then galloped through the mile in 1:35 2/5, leaving the Kentucky hardboots nodding with approval.

This guy could go, but he didn't have to in a bloodless Blue Grass, where he, again at 1-20, stayed outside

his three opponents (Lot o' Gold and Bishop's Choice were back for more) until the backstretch, then sailed away serenely. There was no sudden move, no burst of acceleration, no need for that, really.

Bid and Franklin won by seven lengths in a pedestrian 1:50 for the nine-furlong trip, leading some to question the performance, but Delp was fine with it although he said he would have been okay had they gone faster.

Now it was really and truly show time. The preliminaries were over, and Churchill Downs' twin spires beckoned. There is no more drama in horse racing than the two weeks leading up to the Kentucky Derby, and 1979 would be no different.

# SPECTACULAR BID

# CHAPTER 4

## *The Almost Triple Crown*

F ollowing back-to-back Triple Crowns, the pundits were looking at a possible third straight, with a likely odds-on favorite in Spectacular Bid facing several new shooters, including a long-awaited clash with western rival Flying Paster.

The Gummo colt had snared his 1979 debut in the San Vicente Stakes easily in a quick 1:21 1/5 for seven furlongs, then was upset by a head and a nose in the one and one-sixteenth-mile San Felipe Handicap while giving away tons of weight (he was carrying 127 pounds) six days after a too-fast mile workout.

He got redemption in the Santa Anita Derby, winning by six and a half lengths in 1:48 for nine furlongs, then smashed a solid field in Hollywood Park's Hollywood Derby on April 14, winning by ten lengths with a clocking of 1:47 3/5 for the mile and one-eighth trip.

Those two performances had West Coast horsemen, and many in the East, convinced that he was ready to lower Bid's colors.

Also on hand would be juvenile rival General Assembly, whose three-year-old career had been checkered, beginning with a third-place finish behind Belle's Gold and Screen King in Aqueduct's Swift Stakes. He bounced back to beat that pair in the Gotham Stakes, then was an unsettling fifth to Instrument Landing and Screen King in the Wood Memorial, where he had traffic trouble.

Screen King, a consistent and progressive type, would be at Churchill Downs, along with Lot o' Gold and King Celebrity, a nicely bred longshot (by Personality out of a Bold Ruler mare) who was well beaten by Bid in the Flamingo, but had won the Stepping Stone Purse over the Churchill strip the previous Saturday by ten lengths.

Also on hand was an intriguing youngster named Golden Act, another Gummo colt who had won the Louisiana Derby and Arkansas Derby, the latter over Smarten, a well-regarded Woody Stephens trainee, and Strike the Main, who had been twelve lengths astern of Bid in the Flamingo.

The focus on the Bid-Flying Paster match was such

that Golden Act was virtually ignored, although his form said he had a decent chance.

Delp, though, remained supremely confident in Spectacular Bid and had not been shy all spring about calling his horse "great," a term that trainers usually don't utter about anything they train until well after the horse is retired. He talked openly about winning the Triple Crown and willingly compared his colt — favorably — to Man o' War, Secretariat, Citation, et al.

He wanted to have fun with the moment, and if his style put some people off, there was nothing acrimonious or personally egotistical in his statements. Delp really believed his horse was everything he said he was and wanted everyone else to believe, too.

There was, in fact, little drama about the 105th Kentucky Derby. Bid, breaking from the third post position, dropped off the early pace and was in the two-path in seventh place as the field swept around the first turn.

Given his great tactical speed, many had expected Bid to be closer to the early pace, which was not expected to be fast, but Franklin had him clear, relaxed, and under control going down the backside.

General Assembly, meanwhile, was vying for the

lead with long shot Shamgo through modest early fractions (:24 1/5 for the quarter, :47 2/5 for the half, 1:12 2/5 for six furlongs), with Flying Paster parked not far behind, just ahead of Bid.

The East-West duel everyone was waiting for was about to be joined. Or was it?

As Bid ranged up on Flying Paster and General Assembly on the far turn, Flying Paster came out slightly and brushed the 3-5 favorite, but Franklin said that incident only made his horse "madder," suggesting Bid had on his game face.

By the early stretch, Franklin had his horse on top and heading home. General Assembly kept going steadily while Flying Paster fell back after his bumps with Spectacular Bid. King Celebrity had rallied mildly on the far turn and ran on evenly, while Golden Act came from well back to finish strongly.

None of this really mattered, for the best three-year-old in America was long gone, cruising under the wire with a two and three-quarters-length margin, running the one and a quarter-mile distance in 2:02 2/5 over a fast but dull track. General Assembly was an easy second, Golden Act third, and Flying Paster fifth, beaten ten lengths.

This was a strong, if not overpowering, performance, with the one puzzle being Flying Paster's race. Opinion was divided over whether he didn't handle the track, the distance, or Spectacular Bid. He would get another look in the Preakness, as would Golden Act, Screen King, and General Assembly. No one else would choose to test the Bid on his home ground in Maryland.

Delp, the Meyerhoffs, and Franklin were ecstatic after the Derby, with Delp calling the young rider "a pro," and Harry Meyerhoff likewise expressing satisfaction with Franklin.

Meyerhoff also told the press that while offers had been made to buy the colt for racing and stud purposes, he had no plans to sell or syndicate him, instead hoping to have him around for a four-year-old season.

It was back home to Maryland for the second leg of the Triple Crown and the next step on Bud Delp's road to perfection.

The short, if qualitatively strong, Preakness field led to speculation about the pace of the race with expectations that General Assembly would take the lead, and very possibly, Spectacular Bid would chase him.

Rain on Friday and early Saturday had left the track "good," not much different from Churchill Downs on Derby Day, perhaps a none-too-good harbinger for Flying Paster, who had struggled in Louisville.

When the field broke for the 104th Preakness, Flying Paster, on the inside, came out slightly into Spectacular Bid, and it was Paster who went up to contest the lead with General Assembly.

Spectacular Bid recovered nicely from his brush at the start and settled into fourth behind Screen King (under Cordero), ahead of Golden Act. The leaders bowled along at a faster clip than in the Derby (:23 2/5, :46 4/5), while alternating on the lead.

Franklin, always wanting to stay wide to avoid a Florida Derby rerun, was poised to move outside of Screen King going down the backstretch. Cordero took his mount farther out, perhaps purposely "herding" the 1-10 favorite, but Bid was too much horse for this nonsense and rushed by him at the half-mile pole while surging toward the lead.

He had that lead by a head through six furlongs in 1:10 3/5, then simply drew steadily away from his beaten opponents to a six-length lead in mid-stretch.

Hand-ridden to the wire by Franklin, Bid was the easiest of Preakness winners by five and a half lengths, completing the mile and three-sixteenths in 1:54 1/5, only one-fifth off Canonero II's official Preakness record.

Golden Act finished well again to be a clear second, and Screen King was third after shutting off a tiring Flying Paster in the early stretch. The latter was fourth, beaten eleven lengths by Bid, and a half-length to the good of General Assembly, who, once again, was a disappointment when much more was expected. Bid's win made him a millionaire, with $1,123,587 in earnings.

The winner was, of course, highly popular with the hometown folks, despite a $2.20-$2.20 mutuel payoff (there was no show betting permitted), and by now most people believed the Triple Crown was pretty close to a formality.

Only Golden Act seemed likely to challenge him from the beaten Preakness bunch, and anyone new would have to surface in the three-week interim between the Preakness and Belmont.

Something did, in the form of Coastal, winner of the Peter Pan Stakes in an eye-catching 1:47 for one and one-eighth miles, a supplemental nominee to the Belmont at

a cost of $20,000 to owner William Haggin Perry.

Coastal, a good-looking son of 1969 Kentucky Derby-Preakness winner Majestic Prince out of the Buckpasser mare Alluvial, bred by Claiborne Farm, had the pedigree to be anything, but as a two-year-old had looked pretty ordinary, finishing seventeen lengths behind Bid in the World's Playground Stakes after winning a division of the Tyro Stakes at Monmouth earlier.

The colt injured his eye in his next race, and trainer David Whiteley gave him to his father, Hall of Famer Frank Whiteley, of Damascus and Ruffian fame, for a while before wintering him in California.

At three, the colt had won his three starts, including the Peter Pan, in progressive style for Whiteley. The decision to run in the Belmont, though, was a combination of Coastal's development and Whiteley's thoughts that Bid had not worked particularly well since the Preakness, the gray colt's strenuous year (six races around two turns), and a running strategy (big mid-race moves) that might not suit at one and a half miles.

Still, it was a sporting risk, to say the least, for Perry to put up $20,000 to face a horse who seemed poised for a leap into immortality.

Bid's workouts between the Preakness and Belmont were, indeed, interesting. He breezed seven furlongs in 1:26 at Pimlico on May 31, then shipped to Belmont for final preparations for the June 9 race.

On Monday, June 4, he went out to Belmont's sloppy main track, heavy from several days of persistent rain, and worked a mile around the "dogs" (cones set up well off the rail) in 1:39, galloping out one and one-eighth miles in 1:52 3/5. By contrast, the high-class Greentree Stable gelding Bowl Game, noted for his affinity for wet or soft conditions, did the same work in 1:56 an hour later.

The few people around to note Bid's move saw a fatigued horse going back to the barn, one who had gone through a stiff test, given his rigorous racing schedule of the winter and spring.

Nearly everyone else regarded the work as another example of the gray colt's immense ability and well-being, and he was heavy odds-on to handle Coastal and six others, including Golden Act, Screen King, King Celebrity, and General Assembly, who trainer LeRoy Jolley had earlier said would not chase Bid for a while.

The track was fast, although somewhat deep, after

having been resurfaced the previous fall, and Franklin, who had an altercation with Cordero after an overnight race earlier in the week, was keen to prove his horse superior in the way of, say, Secretariat.

Gallant Best jumped out to an early lead and set what were very fast fractions for a mile and a half race: :23 2/5, :47 3/5, and 1:11 1/5 for six furlongs at which point Spectacular Bid went to the lead.

Bid was where his connections wanted him to be, clear and winging on the front end of the Belmont, through a mile in 1:36 (equaling the third-fastest mile ever), racing to history. He got to the quarter pole in 2:02 2/5 with a three-length lead, but moving with purpose just behind him were Ruben Hernandez and Coastal, cutting inside Bid, moving better than the champ, decisively driving by him!

In a few strides, it was evident that Bid's twelve-race win streak would end, and Franklin was bringing back a tired horse.

Coastal won by three and a quarter lengths, and the steady, consistent Golden Act got second by a neck over a gallant Bid, who rallied mildly when challenged by Golden Act.

What had happened to the "greatest horse to ever look through a bridle"? Was the distance too much, had he been moved too quickly, not allowing for the extra quarter-mile grind of the Belmont, or was he simply "over the top" after months of dominating performances?

Delp, to his credit, accepted the defeat with aplomb, said Franklin had performed well, and left Belmont subdued, but with his head up.

There was, however, to be another angle to this story, one that would surface after Delp returned to Maryland. There he said that on Belmont morning he arrived at the barn to find the colt's groom, Mo Hall, anguished.

Hall told him that Bid had "stepped on a pin," which turned out to be a safety pin of the type used to hold together protective leg wrappings. Bid was said to chew on his wraps, raising the possibility that he pulled loose a pin and stepped on it.

Delp said he found the pin imbedded in the colt's left front foot and the colt was gimpy. He pulled the pin out, squeezed the hoof, walked then jogged Bid in the shedrow (the colt showed no sign of lameness), talked to the Meyerhoffs and New York Racing Association veterinarian Dr. Manuel Gilman, and decided to send his horse over for the Belmont, assuming no further complications. Harry Meyerhoff would later say, "We thought about not running, but Bud said he didn't think the foot was bothering him. I believe it did affect him in the race, because he wouldn't change leads, which is almost unheard of in a race that long."

There were, certainly, cynics who decided this was simply a convenient post-race excuse for a stunning loss, but this made little sense, because those who were involved verified Delp's account of things and no mention of the safety pin was made post-race. Others suggested that the problem was something other than a safety pin, perhaps a chronic injury resurfacing, and Delp's sometimes conspiratorial, "just having fun with you" style didn't help his credibility.

Regardless, the colt, shipped to Delaware Park the morning after the Belmont, was quite lame by that afternoon. That he had an injury to the foot in question was evident, and Dr. Alex Harthill, the famed Louisville vet, flew in to see what he could find.

He found infected laminae, which he drained and treated, after which farrier Jack Reynolds put on a padded shoe to protect the injury from further risk of infection.

Bid would be on the shelf for a while, although Delp was already talking about the Jim Dandy and Travers, both part of the historic Saratoga late summer meeting, as targets for the colt, in whom he was still supremely confident.

The Belmont and his mid-week skirmish with Cordero had raised fresh questions about Franklin's maturity, and a mid-June arrest at Disneyland for alleged cocaine possession led the Meyerhoffs and Delp to replace him permanently with Bill Shoemaker, although Delp would continue to use Franklin on his other horses while the charge was being investigated.

For Franklin, the permanent loss of the ride of his life would become part of a pattern that would eventually drive him from the racetrack, a sad tale of substance abuse and denial that would destroy a meteoric career.

Those who were tired of Delp's audacious claims on behalf of his horse and who thought Ronnie Franklin was an accident waiting to happen would have their moments in the summer of '79, for Delp was quiet and Franklin in trouble.

Spectacular Bid, too, was having a quiet summer,

although Claiborne Farm president Seth Hancock announced he and the Meyerhoffs had reached an agreement that Bid would stand at Claiborne after his retirement from racing. While no details were discussed publicly, it was evident that the Meyerhoffs intended to continue running him at three and keep him in training at four, health and form permitting.

His form was never at issue, but his health was, and when Delp got him back to galloping at Delaware Park in early July, the colt was still not ready to put severe pressure on that left front foot. In fact, says Harry Meyerhoff, "We had a very big concern that he might not be able to come back, after the piece of his foot that Dr. Harthill had to cut away."

There were the usual rumors that all was not well and he might never race again, but Bid worked three furlongs in :35 4/5 in late July, then a half in :49, signaling he was on the right road.

If the Belmont raised questions about his superiority over other members of his generation, the colt was without peer as a lover of jelly doughnuts.

Once Bid's taste in doughnuts was established, he and Delp played a little game following the horse's morning visits to the racetrack. While Bid was walking in the shedrow, Delp would hide in a tack room, jelly doughnut in hand. Bid soon figured out the source of the doughnuts, and would stop and peer into the tack room, waiting for Delp — and the doughnuts — to come forth.

By mid-August, Delp was looking for an allowance race for his colt's return, and on August 26 Spectacular Bid and new associate Bill Shoemaker went postward against four other unwitting steeds in a one and one-sixteenth-mile overnight at Delaware.

The track had some water in it from earlier rains, but Bid was unfazed, tracking the early pace, then sweeping by the leader on the turn and storming away to win by seventeen lengths in track-record time of 1:41 3/5.

He beat nothing, and the race was obscure, but his effort was flawless, even scintillating, and racing fans across America looked forward to his dust-up with 1978 Triple Crown winner Affirmed in Belmont's Marlboro Cup on September 8.

Also possible for the race were Coastal, winner since the Belmont of the Dwyer Stakes and the Monmouth Invitational in early August, and General Assembly, fresh from a spectacular fifteen-length victory in the Travers Stakes at Saratoga in a track record 2:00 for ten furlongs. When he was good, General Assembly was very good.

It was the Bid-Affirmed confrontation, though, that stirred imaginations. It also stirred New York racing secretary Lenny Hale to assign Affirmed 133 pounds for the Marlboro Cup, a handicap, versus 124 for the three-year-old; nine pounds of actual weight and four above scale (at scale weights the two would have carried 126 and 121, respectively).

Trainer Laz Barrera, who had taken Affirmed through three years of success at the highest levels of racing and was as confident in his charge as was Delp in Spectacular Bid, was — how to phrase this? — livid with Hale's weights and said so in colorful, sometimes indecipherable terms.

He also said Affirmed would not run, and any meeting with Bid would have to come in either the Woodward Stakes or Jockey Club Gold Cup.

That being that, the Marlboro was still going to be something special, with the season's best three-year-olds settling their differences against a stellar group of older horses such as Metropolitan and Whitney Handicap winner Star de Naskra; Text, recent winner of the Haskell Handicap at Monmouth; and multiple graded-stakes winner Cox's Ridge.

This was the best field yet faced by Spectacular Bid, and with only the Delaware allowance win, albeit impressive, under his girth since his Belmont disappointment and subsequent injury, there had to be questions about his fitness.

The Belmont crowd shrugged off such concerns, showing their confidence in the mottled gray by sending him off as the 1-2 favorite.

General Assembly quickly took the lead, then handed off to Star de Naskra, the two of them tag teaming through moderate early fractions, with Spectacular Bid just behind them.

They reached a half-mile in :47 2/5 just as Shoemaker sent Bid after them, and as he rolled by, Delp told Harry Meyerhoff, "This race is history. He'll win."

Shoemaker hit the gray once and showed him the stick the rest of the way, which was a Spectacular Bid ticker-tape parade to the winner's circle. He came to the finish in front by five lengths over General Assembly, who was second by one and a quarter lengths over Coastal. The time was a superb 1:46 3/5, best time of the year by a three-year-old for nine furlongs.

His Marlboro Cup win settled a score with Coastal, continued his mastery of General Assembly, and pushed his record to sixteen wins in nineteen starts and earnings of $1,346,667, with $962,183 acquired in 1979 alone, a single season record.

Bid was not only well established as the top three-year-old in the land, but positioned to challenge Affirmed for Horse of the Year honors.

Affirmed had been 1978 Horse of the Year after a strange fall campaign that saw him lose squarely to 1977 Triple Crown winner Seattle Slew in the Marlboro Cup, then finish behind Slew again in the Jockey Club Gold Cup when Affirmed's saddle slipped. There were many who believed Slew was the better horse that fall, but Affirmed's Triple Crown heroics carried enough water to earn him the ultimate title.

He had lost twice at Santa Anita in the winter of '79, but won the Strub Stakes, Santa Anita Handicap, Californian Stakes, and Hollywood Gold Cup in exceptional style afterward.

The Woodward, at ten furlongs on September 24, was probably more eagerly awaited than had been the Marlboro Cup, given Bid's spectacular performance in the latter, and Coastal was also being sent out to try both horses.

This time, however, it was Bid's turn to defect after he developed a slight fever a few days before the Woodward. Observations were made that this was actually Delp's way of one-upping Barrera for not running in the Marlboro Cup, but Delp said he, in fact, would prefer facing Affirmed at one and a quarter miles in the Woodward than in the one and a half-mile Jockey Club Gold Cup fourteen days later.

In Bid's absence, Affirmed beat Coastal by two and a half lengths.

Finally, after weeks of talking and sparring, the great summit would occur on Saturday, October 6, 1979, in the $350,000 Jockey Club Gold Cup. This weight-for-age event, in pre-Breeders' Cup days, was the closest American equivalent to France's Prix de l'Arc de Triomphe, Europe's most important weight-for-age test.

Affirmed bounced quickly from the gate, but jockey Laffit Pincay Jr. let Gallant Best have the early lead, with a slower breaking Bid third, Coastal next to him. Bid had to be steadied slightly just after the break, but was soon traveling smoothly chasing Affirmed, who had gone to the front after a :25 first quarter.

Affirmed continued to lead down the backstretch and into the turn, staying well off the rail on a drying out racetrack. Pincay asked him for some run on the turn, and Bid actually lost ground to the older horse.

Meanwhile, as they turned for home, Coastal made his bid on the inside, and he drew alongside Affirmed at one point, perhaps even gaining the narrowest of leads.

But Affirmed would have none of it, edging away from the Majestic Prince colt. Shoemaker, gathering his horse again, changed course slightly to get between Affirmed and Coastal and take aim on the leader.

So here it was, three-sixteenths of a mile to go and the winners of the last six Triple Crown races stretched out in full flight, one of those rare moments when all the good things about racing come together at once.

Bid pushed past Coastal into second place and got to Affirmed's saddle towel as those two were driving to the wire under Shoemaker and Pincay at their best. Affirmed would edge away, Bid would battle back.

Affirmed wouldn't give in, Bid wouldn't give up; the irresistible force had met the immovable object.

This was a struggle of titans, and in the end, the older titan proved best by three-quarters of length, finishing in 2:27 2/5, the final quarter in :25. Coastal was third, three lengths back of Bid. Harry Meyerhoff said that Shoemaker told him later that he had not recognized how slow the pace was and failed to go on as quickly as he should have.

Regardless, Affirmed was the best, if only just so, and Bid had proved that he could handle a mile and a half, under conditions that probably were more favorable to Affirmed. He also solidified his superiority over Coastal, who, nonetheless, also proved his mettle against two of the best horses in American racing memory.

Coastal and Affirmed would soon be retired, but Delp was still looking for another outing for Spectacular Bid, and after toying around with the idea of trying him on the grass in the Washington, D.C., International (there also was talk of Affirmed going there), Delp decided on the Meadowlands Cup, also $350,000-added over one and a quarter miles, twelve days after the Gold Cup.

Delp's decision to go to the Meadowlands was not solely based on the desire to close out the year with a win. Affirmed's first-place prize in the Gold Cup had pushed him past Bid as the all-time leading single season money earner, and Delp, always the competitor, wanted that record back. Meadowlands management nudged the decision along with a $100,000 bump to the $250,000 base purse.

Sometimes these "afterthought" races at the end of the season backfire when fresh challengers appear to face the erstwhile stars, and Bid ended up meeting four-time Derby winner Smarten (Ohio, Illinois, Pennsylvania, and American Derbies, second in General Assembly's Travers) and the much-touted Valdez, a stablemate of Affirmed and also a son of leading sire Exclusive Native.

Valdez had wins over the Meadowlands strip in the Rutgers and Paterson Handicaps and would carry 121 pounds, five less than Bid and one less than Smarten. Text, carrying 117, and King Celebrity, with 112, completed the field.

Text, under Cordero, went to the lead quickly with Bid and Valdez tracking him. Shoemaker moved Bid to the outside to keep him away from any traffic problems inside and to keep an eye on Valdez, the horse he thought they had to beat.

Valdez tackled Text going into the far turn and they vied for the lead around the turn with Valdez gradually edging ahead. But the 1-10 favorite was lurking on the outside, and when Shoemaker tapped him a few times to remind him of his task, Bid went smoothly to the lead. Shoemaker said afterward that he moved "earlier than I really wanted because Valdez was running so easy."

Valdez staged a brief rally, but Bid was home free, easing off to a three-length win over Smarten, who pipped Valdez by a head for second. Bid's final time of 2:01 1/5 was a new track record by two-fifths of a second.

The victory was anticlimactic but lucrative. The $234,650 first prize boosted Bid's 1979 earnings to $1,279,334, moving past Affirmed's $1,148,800 recently established tally set in the Jockey Club Gold Cup. Spectacular Bid completed his high-wire act season with ten wins in twelve starts, one second, and one third. After two years his tally was seventeen for twenty-one, with $1,663,818 in earnings, placing him fifth on the all-time career earnings list.

For Delp, the year had gone as remarkably as he had

predicted, or probably hoped, it would. Bid had proved himself to be the versatile, dominating performer Delp said he would be, and respect for the colt was very high among horsemen and Turf writers as the year ended.

While opinions varied on the reasons for his Belmont loss, Bid's fall comeback validated the view that he was a horse well up to the standards of Triple Crown winners, a special talent to be mentioned in the same breath with Affirmed, Seattle Slew, Forego, Alydar, and, yes, even Secretariat.

He was unanimous choice as three-year-old champion male and runner-up to Affirmed in Horse of the Year voting. Delp, fourth among North American trainers in stable earnings, soon announced that Bid's four-year-old career would commence at Santa Anita, where he would contest the Strub series for four-year-olds — the Malibu, San Fernando, and Strub Stakes and the Santa Anita Handicap.

Bid had been brilliant at two, nearly unbeatable at three, but the barnstorming tour Delp had in mind for him in 1980 would serve as a platform for greatness.

## *The Safest Wager*

T he Eclipse Award for best three-year-old male was not the only Eclipse in which Spectacular Bid figured.

The photographic award was presented to Skip Ball, the now-deceased photographic director for *The Maryland Horse* magazine. The photo captured Bid's "flying" finish in the Kentucky Derby and was one of those rare pictures of a horse with all four feet off the ground simultaneously. It was a perfect moment and a precursor to a racing year that began and ended perfectly for the gray son of Bold Bidder and Spectacular.

Some thought that Bid might be retired to Claiborne, despite previous public pronouncements to the contrary, following his win in the Meadowlands Cup. He had, after all, done just about everything a horse could do up to that point except win the Triple

Crown, which was now beyond his grasp, and capture Horse of the Year honors.

The path of history is littered with horses that have been stars at two and three, only to have their luck run out at four, when wear, tear, and the burden of giving away weight in handicaps compromises glittering records. There have been occasional suggestions that the most important older-horse races be made weight-for-age in order to put every competitor on a level playing field.

Of course, this would lead to short fields, given the number of options available to American horsemen, in many of the country's showcase events, but purists contend that this is only fair to the superstar horses and to the fans, who like to see such horses win.

American racing, though, has always operated with a standard that says the best of the breed are precocious at two, classic winners at three, and premier weight carriers at four or beyond.

Bid's value, as an economic matter, would be established in the spring of 1980 when Claiborne president Seth Hancock syndicated the horse for a then-record $550,000 per share, with a forty-share deal, thus making him the first-ever $22 million horse. With syndication values inevitably climbing at about the national inflation rate but more or less in lock step with the average price at the Keeneland and Saratoga summer yearling sales, Bid's share price represented a quantum jump, perhaps portending the same leap in select yearling averages.

Betting on him as a stallion prospect was a calculated gamble. Betting on him as a racehorse would turn out to be 1980's safest wager.

The four-year-old Spectacular Bid, reappearing first at four on January 5, 1980, in the Malibu Stakes at Santa Anita, was, according to Bud Delp, an improvement over the 1979 model. He had been measured at 15 hands, 3 1/4 inches the previous fall, but Delp said he was a bit over 16 hands now and had added weight and muscle.

A deep-girthed colt with the strong, well-angled shoulder typical of the Nearco-line horses, Bid was cold steel compared with the round apples that so often catch the eye of Thoroughbred admirers, but it was the steel of a bayonet.

The Malibu was stripped down to five starters with Bid in the gate. One of the other four was a rejuvenated Flying Paster, fresh, fit, on his home ground, and in receipt of three pounds from Bid, who carried top

weight of 126. A crowd of 46,948 showed up to watch the renewal of the rivalry and bet Bid down to 3-10.

Harry Meyerhoff remembers an amusing moment that accentuated for him his colt's popularity. "There was a big crowd in the paddock before the race and around the outside. Some loud guy — I don't know if he was drunk or what — yelled, 'Why don't you go back home. Those eastern so-and-so's can't run.' Another guy yelled back, 'Don't listen to him. We love Bid.' "

Shoemaker, knowing this seven-furlong race would be run rapidly, wanted to keep his horse in contact with the pace. Bid was off in his usual moderate way and settled in behind the leaders in last place but never more than a few lengths off the pace, which was carved out by Rosie's Seville.

The latter ripped through the opening quarter in :22 1/5 and found himself being dogged by Don Pierce aboard Flying Paster, who had saved ground along the rail. Shoemaker, watching his rival closely, soon asked Bid to join the leaders, which he did in the middle of the final turn, the half-mile run in :44 2/5.

At the head of the stretch, Bid was four wide but in high gear, with Flying Paster digging in to challenge along the inside. The battle was joined. Or was it?

The Shoe tapped his gray companion once with the whip, and the result was an afterburner jolt that quickly placed daylight between them and Flying Paster, a distance that grew to five lengths at the wire. Bid roared by the eighth pole in 1:08 for six furlongs, and under a hand ride, stopped the teletimer in 1:20, a new Santa Anita record, only a fifth of a second off Triple Bend's world record for the distance.

In a town that places a high value on glitz, this was a headliner performance, one hailed with head-shaking enthusiasm by local Turf writers and horsemen. Flying Paster's race, given his seven-month layoff, was quite good, and the two were confirmed as contestants in the next leg of the Strub Series, the one and one-eighth mile San Fernando Stakes on January 19.

Delp, ever cautious, told reporters he would see them in the press box after the San Fernando. He didn't do much with his horse between the two races, probably because of swelling in the colt's left front ankle right after the Malibu. There was no fracture, but X-rays showed a strain of the ligament on the inside of the sesamoid.

Called by his trainer "the greatest horse ever to look through a bridle," Spectacular Bid did his best to live up to the praise, dominating his peers at two, three, and four.

California owner-breeders Mrs. William M. Jason (left) and her mother, Mrs. William G. Gilmore (right), bred Spectacular Bid in Kentucky and later sold the colt as a yearling (above) at the 1977 Keeneland September sale to the Meyerhoffs.

Brilliance both on the track
and at stud made Bold Ruler
(above) a tough act for his
sons to follow. Bold Bidder
(left) did his best, becoming
a champion handicap horse
and consistent sire, with
Spectacular Bid being by far
his best offspring.

Spectacular Bid's broodmare
sire, Promised Land (left),
was a solid stakes horse who
passed on his gray color to
his grandson through his
stakes-placed daughter,
Spectacular (below).

Spectacular Bid was surrounded by several colorful characters, including (facing page, clockwise from top right) his outspoken trainer, Bud Delp; brash young rider Ronnie Franklin; and brilliant veteran jockey Bill Shoemaker.

Also in Bid's circle of human connections were his owners Tom Meyerhoff (above left) and Teresa and Harry Meyerhoff (above center holding the Kentucky Derby trophy), and his groom, Herman (Mo) Hall (left).

Bid's first stakes win came in the World's Playground at Atlantic City (top). He then added victories in the Champagne (right) and Young America (above on rail), both grade I races. Jockey Jorge Velasquez (right aboard Bid) replaced Franklin for the Champagne and Young America.

Ronnie Franklin was back aboard as Bid closed out his two-year-old campaign with easy scores in the Laurel Futurity (right) and the Heritage Stakes at Keystone (below).

Driving rain didn't deter Bid from winning his three-year-old debut, the Hutcheson, in hand (above). Continuing on the Triple Crown trail, Bid had no trouble winning the Fountain of Youth, Florida Derby (below), and Flamingo Stakes (left) before leaving Florida for Kentucky.

Local media greeted Spectacular Bid when he arrived at Blue Grass Airfield in Lexington to prepare for his final Kentucky Derby prep, the Blue Grass Stakes at Keeneland. Bid didn't miss a beat, winning the race by seven lengths (above).

Spectacular Bid went to post (bottom) in the Kentucky Derby as the odds-on favorite and won as he pleased. (Bid's Derby win photo, below, taken by Skip Ball, received the 1979 Eclipse Award for photography.) The Preakness was even easier (opposite, below left), and after the race (opposite, below right), it seemed like nothing could stop Bid from becoming the 12th Triple Crown winner, the fourth of that decade. However, a safety pin and a horse named Coastal helped contribute to the unthinkable — Bid lost the Belmont (opposite, top) and the Triple Crown.

Bid, now partnered with Bill Shoemaker, showed he was back from his Belmont defeat by demolishing an allowance field by seventeen lengths and romping by five in the Marlboro Cup (left). After a tough loss to 1978 Triple Crown winner Affirmed in the Jockey Club Gold Cup, Bid earned some down time (bottom). He then took the Meadowlands Cup (below) for his final start of the year.

Spectacular Bid's perfect four-year-old season began in California where his average margin of victory in six starts was nearly four and a half lengths. Among his wins were the Californian (above), Santa Anita Handicap (right), and San Fernando Stakes (below).

Bid ventured out of California in the summer of 1980 to win the Washington Park Handicap (right) by ten lengths and the Amory L. Haskell Handicap (above) ridden out by one and three-quarters lengths.

Bid's dominance at four cul-
minated in a rare "walkover"
in the Woodward Stakes
when no one would run
against him. Bid started alone
and finished alone — a fairly
regular sight even when he
had competition.

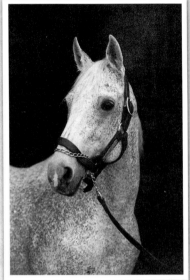

Although not the brilliant sire everyone had hoped, Spectacular Bid has sired several nice runners, including grade I winner Spectacular Love (above) and multiple stakes winner Double Feint (below). Bid, at the age of twenty-five in 2001, was standing at stud at Milfer Farm in upstate New York.

Bid was treated with hot and cold wraps, and the swelling disappeared. Still, Delp gave him no serious speed work before the San Fernando, which would be run on a drying racetrack that began the day rated slow and was later upgraded to good.

Flying Paster, fitter than before, and the fast and versatile Relaunch also were entered in the San Fernando, along with Timbo, who would be around to collect fourth money.

Bid, at 1-20, caused a Santa Anita record minus show pool of $85,026.55, and for a few moments in the stretch, his backers had something to be anxious about.

He did his usual back-to-last routine after the break, with Relaunch jumping into the lead, followed by Timbo and Flying Paster. The latter dropped back rounding the first turn, as if he did not like the going.

Meanwhile, as they rushed down the backside, Bid surged up to challenge Relaunch, moving on his own while Shoe tried to keep him relaxed.

They raced with Relaunch into the turn, then Bid went to the front, but Flying Paster had found his best action again and was moving quickly on the outside, closing on Bid.

A bigger, longer-striding colt, Flying Paster had the crowd on its feet with the power of his move, and he was showing no signs of losing momentum in mid-stretch. Shoemaker was concerned about the Gummo colt's move and dug in to fend off a very serious challenge.

Asked for more, Bid found it and drew off slowly, winning by a length and a half, most of that advantage gained in the final hundred yards. The time was 1:48, good under the conditions, better when one considered the talented Relaunch was beaten sixteen and a half lengths.

The San Fernando might have been a good win by a great horse not quite at his best, but for Flying Paster fans, it was an uplifting day, leaving a hint of something better to come.

Would that better day come in the Strub Series finale on February 3, the ten-furlong Charles H. Strub Stakes? Weights would be more favorable to Flying Paster (121 pounds versus 126 on Bid), and Valdez, a testy adversary for Bid in the '79 Meadowlands Cup would be on hand to add competitive drama. Flying Paster would reinforce his backers' expectations with a phenomenal mile workout in 1:35 2/5 five days before the Strub.

Nevertheless, Delp was confident — what else? — that his horse would be better in the Strub.

On a glib racing surface, Relaunch flew into the lead and made fractions more like those in a Quarter Horse match race instead of a mile and a quarter test of champions.

He reached the quarter in :22, the half in :44 3/5, and six furlongs in 1:08 2/5, opening a ten-length lead at one point. Bid, though, was on the warpath heading toward the far turn, with Valdez and Laffit Pincay determined not to let him slip away uncontested. The three raced as a team through the turn, with Bid gaining a slight advantage after the mile in 1:32 4/5.

Flying Paster, who had trailed early, was on his game again and found room inside Valdez to come after Bid. As in the San Fernando, he was resolute throughout the stretch, running a winning race. The problem was that the gray stiletto in front of him had, at Shoemaker's request, found another gear and was gone again, coming to the wire three and a half lengths ahead of Flying Paster, who had nine on Valdez.

A record Strub crowd of 57,993 roared its appreciation for Spectacular Bid's show of class, then blew apart the applause meter when the impact of the final time was realized. Spectacular Bid had run one and a quarter miles in 1:57 4/5, a new stakes, track, and world record on a dirt surface. He broke the old world mark by two-fifths of a second and left even the understated Shoe startled, almost effusive: "He's a great horse, at least as good as I've ever ridden, maybe better — I don't know what it'll take to beat this horse." Shoe said every time he touched the horse with the whip, he delivered another move.

Shoemaker had just won his 7,784th career race. None had been more spectacular.

Delp, himself a bit in awe of what he'd seen, said the colt might run in the San Antonio Stakes on February 17, two weeks later and the same distance in front of his main goal, the Santa Anita Handicap.

The San Antonio, however, was bypassed, and Bid was given 130 pounds for the Big 'Cap, Santa Anita's proudest tradition and a day management was hoping to draw 60,000 or more to see the crowning of the king of California.

Flying Paster, assigned 123 pounds, and the fleet Beau's Eagle, who had won the San Antonio impressively, were among the four horses mustered to face

Bid. The only possible hiccup for him appeared to be the weather, with local forecasts calling for rain showers and a probable sloppy track, which Delp maintained the horse did not like.

The forecasts were wrong, but in an unfortunate way. The showers came, but they went from light to heavy with gusting winds by mid-morning, and conditions did not improve all day. It was a chilly, wet day that greeted Bid, Flying Paster, and the others in the paddock, where it seemed most of the strong crowd of 49,285 assembled to see the Big 'Cap field parade.

It was noted that Bid was not wearing mud caulks, as were the other four starters, but Delp said he never considered using the "sticker" shoes. Instead, he said he talked with Shoemaker regularly through the afternoon about the track's condition and acknowledged he considered scratching, but decided to leave him in the race because he believed in his horse, and he didn't want to disappoint the crowd.

The trainer and jockey saw Beau's Eagle as the speed of the race and decided to stay in touch with him from the start, not wanting to risk one of those patented front-running wet-track jobs by a speed horse.

Beau's Eagle did his part by going to the front, then backing up the pace. He went the quarter in :24 2/5 and the half in :48 3/5, building a four-length lead after six furlongs in 1:12 2/5, with Spectacular Bid sitting in second, watching and waiting.

Shoemaker "sent" his horse at the half-mile pole and was quickly alongside Beau's Eagle, with old pal Flying Paster ranging up alongside and moving powerfully. Would this be a rerun of the San Fernando? Would the wet track undo Bid?

No and no.

Two taps of Shoemaker's whip set him alight, and it was sayonara to Flying Paster and Beau's Eagle. After what was, by his standards, a tepid mile in 1:36 4/5, Bid ran his final quarter in :23 4/5 with no pressure. His final time of 2:00 3/5, on a tiring track under 130 pounds, was excellent, and he joined Seabiscuit, Thumbs Up, Mark-Ye-Well, Round Table, and Ack Ack as the only horses to win the Big 'Cap under that impost up to that time.

This facile victory was his twenty-first in twenty-five career starts and pushed his earnings to $2,089,418, just over $300,000 less than the all-time leading money earner, Affirmed.

Delp thought the race was Bid's best, most dominating performance at Santa Anita and considering the
conditions, he might well have been right. Shoemaker
simply said, "Bid is about as good as any horse you'll
ever see."

Best horse to ever look though a bridle. Hmm,
maybe the man had a point.

Spectacular Bid had done exactly what his connections had set out to do with him, which was to conquer
Santa Anita, and in so doing, defeat the best older
horses in training.

Delp's plans for the rest of the year, though, were
scarcely less ambitious. Bid would run two or three
times in California, aiming at the Hollywood Gold
Cup in late June. Then there was a possible trip to
Chicago, followed by the Whitney at Saratoga, then
New York's Fall Championship Series: the Marlboro
Cup, Woodward Stakes, and Jockey Club Gold Cup.
Then, all being well, he would finish matters in the
Meadowlands Cup. This was not just an ambitious
schedule; it was numbing. But, this was a numbing-
ly good horse, seemingly up to any test conceived by
mankind.

Rested after his triumphal march through Santa Anita, Spectacular Bid returned to the races on May 18 in the Mervyn LeRoy Handicap and found that his only real competition left in California was Eual Wyatt Jr., racing secretary at Hollywood Park.

Wyatt, able to see as well as any man, had witnessed the carnage at Santa Anita and had little choice but to try and make things more competitive by the only means available: weight.

He assigned Spectacular Bid 132 pounds for the LeRoy, giving Flying Paster 122, Beau's Eagle 121, and all other would-be starters considerably less.

Delp didn't complain, and Shoemaker and "the gray streak," as Bid was referred to by another trainer, stepped forth in front of 44,836 fans, who bet him down to 1-5.

Bid broke slowly and dropped to the back of the six-horse field, but soon warmed to his task and went on the attack. He ripped off a quarter in :22 3/5 heading down the backstretch to run by everybody but Beau's Eagle, and after a breather, he went after him.

Beau's Eagle tried, briefly, to run with him, but succumbed to Bid's second move and watched the gray's hindquarters distance themselves even farther. At the wire, Bid, following a final mid-stretch burst, was seven lengths ahead of Peregrinator, clocking 1:40 2/5 for one and one-sixteenth miles, four-fifths of a second better than Affirmed the year before in the same race carrying two fewer pounds than the gray. More importantly, he was now only $184,000 short of Affirmed's earnings record.

Next was the June 8 Californian Stakes, a nine-furlong race for which he would be assigned 130 pounds.

Spectacular Bid trained perfectly for the race, but gave Delp an unwanted cheap thrill on the morning of the event when he grabbed the quarter (or back) of his right forefoot, opening a small cut and ripping off his shoe. Delp cleaned up the wound and called farrier Jack Reynolds to fly in from Detroit to replace the shoe, a bit of overkill. In fact, Reynolds couldn't get a commercial flight, so he was told to charter a private jet for $9,000.

This misadventure wasn't over. Reynolds' plane was forced to land in Colorado due to turbulent conditions, so Delp had to settle for a local blacksmith, who replaced the shoe about a half-hour before the race.

In fact, Bid probably could have done without the shoe, for he manhandled a moderate field as he should have and rumbled to a track-record 1:45 4/5 clocking for one and one-eighth miles, lowering by two-fifths of a second the track mark set by the fleet Rich Cream only two races before. The winner's purse of $184,450 eased him by Affirmed and into first place on the money-earning list with $2,394,268. There was more to come.

The track had been decidedly sharp on Californian Day, a fact noted by Delp with some discomfort. Although the Hollywood Gold Cup had long been on the trainer's agenda, he cited the track's condition as his reason for bypassing the Gold Cup and shipping off to Chicago instead. Most observers believed the possibility of a big weight bump for the Gold Cup also might have influenced Delp or possibly concern over a flare-up of that winter ankle injury. Harry Meyerhoff says the Bid camp was concerned over the "hard racetracks" in California, which he feels contributed to the ankle problems that would surface in late fall.

Regardless, the gray colt went to the Windy City to await the Washington Park Stakes on July 19.

It should be noted that the Washington Park Stakes had been the Washington Park Handicap on all but one occasion in fifty-two prior runnings, but Arlington

Park, with a clever eye to promotion, changed the conditions to attract the best horse in the world.

The race nominally carried a $125,000-added purse, but management decided it would be $250,000 if winners of the Kentucky Derby, Preakness, or Belmont started. Bid would get 130 pounds to carry for nine furlongs, and his presence would bump the purse, as was intended.

He arrived at Arlington on July 3 to treatment that bordered on obscene.

The horse got the best straw available, bottled water, a stall with no horses on either side, and a personal security guard around the clock. The only things missing were television and beer, but Delp, who got even better treatment with a room at the Arlington Hilton and a camper at the barn with ample food and beverage supplies plus a cook, told reporters that Bid was getting Pepto Bismol with his oats.

Presumably, this was not considered performance enhancing, even though it supposedly helped the colt avoid a tendency to colic, but it made for good media material in the days leading up to the race.

Bid helped himself in that regard with his workouts, beginning with five furlongs in :58 2/5 on July 7. Soothed by the Pepto, he came back on July 12 with 1:36 4/5 for a mile, then did :46 for a half-mile five days later.

His five opponents, in what was a Spectacular Bid Invitational of sorts, were a reasonable collection of stakes types, the best being Hold Your Tricks, a multiple black-type winner fresh from a victory in Ak-Sar-Ben's Cornhusker Handicap over the classy Overskate.

Spectacular Bid, as was his wont, broke belatedly and was fourth of six turning down the backside, with Hold Your Tricks running on the front end and carving out good fractions (:23 1/5, :46 1/5).

After a half-mile, Shoemaker angled Bid to the outside and let him move to the leader on his own. He was alongside Hold Your Tricks racing through the far turn, then eased ahead as they began turning toward the homestretch.

After that, it was merely a matter of margin, with Bid leading through six furlongs in 1:09 4/5 and steadily drawing away under a hand ride by Shoe. He was five lengths in front at the eighth pole, ten on top at the wire, stopping the clock in 1:46 1/5, a new track record by three-fifths of a second and the eighth track record set by the horse in twenty-eight starts.

Almost 30,000 people had come to Arlington to see the Spectacular Bid traveling road show, and he had been everything they could have expected.

With the heartland having seen greatness on the hoof, Delp announced that (1) he had expected his horse to set a track record, and (2) Bid would next start in the Amory L. Haskell Handicap at Monmouth Park on August 16, assuming he was healthy and the weight spreads were reasonable.

The decision to take Bid to Monmouth was slightly curious, although keeping within the "tour of America" theme being followed. Harry Meyerhoff's wife, Teresa, originally from upstate New York, had suggested running the horse at Saratoga, and in the first part of the year the Whitney Stakes on August 2 was on his schedule.

Harry Meyerhoff says, "He really wasn't ready to run in the Whitney right after the Chicago race. The people in Chicago and at Monmouth were really terrific to us, letting us know how much they wanted us to come, while we never heard from anyone in New York about the Whitney. Monmouth really wanted us."

Delp would later say that the inability to use the anti-inflammatory medication phenylbutazone in New

York influenced his thinking, but his willingness to run Bid at Belmont Park in the fall seemed to cast doubt on that thought.

Other factors more likely to have mattered were the willingness of Monmouth Park management to bump the Haskell purse to $250,000-added to get Bid and what appeared to be a softer field in New Jersey. Delp hadn't ducked challenges in the past, but he said after the Californian that the horse had "absolutely nothing left to prove" and going out against quality horses while giving away tons of weight would, well, prove nothing.

Bid was assigned 132 pounds for the Haskell by racing secretary Kenny Lenox, giving fifteen to twenty-two pounds to his seven rivals.

Most accomplished of the group and closest to Bid in the weights was the high-class Canadian-based filly Glorious Song, a four-year-old by Halo out of the Herbager mare Ballade (the same mating would later produce champion two-year-old Devil's Bag and more recently top young sire Saint Ballado).

Owned by Nelson Bunker Hunt, whose racing empire stretched around the globe, and Canadian businessman Frank Stronach, then relatively new to rac-

ing, Glorious Song was a multiple grade I winner against other distaffers. Hunt, however, had always followed adventuresome policies with his best fillies, and Glorious Song had three stakes wins over males in her trophy collection. Carrying 117 actual pounds (120 if the three-pound sex allowance was considered), she appeared armed and dangerous.

Spectacular Bid was the 1-9 favorite when the gates opened in front of 27,843 fans, and he followed the basic Bid formula: break at his leisure, settle in behind the front-enders, and move on the turn.

Shoemaker and Delp had decided that Glorious Song represented their only possible threat in the Haskell. Shoe decided to track the Halo filly, move when she moved, then reel her in during the stretch drive.

The tactic worked, but a bit more slowly than Bid's fans, especially those who helped create the $81,625 minus show pool by betting heavily on him to show, would have hoped.

Glorious Song was all racehorse and as game as they come. When she made her run at the leaders on the final turn, she did so with lingering strength.

She took the lead in early stretch, with Bid about a

length off her and striving to get by. Shoemaker hit him once with his whip, and the colt edged by the filly, going a half-length up at the eighth pole, a mile run in 1:35 3/5.

Afterward, he opened up some daylight, finishing one and three-quarters lengths ahead of Glorious Song, his final time being 1:48 for nine furlongs. He had been challenged by a hickory race mare in receipt of fifteen pounds and had come through comfortably, if not in the dominant way always expected of him.

The Marlboro Cup, scene of one of Spectacular Bid's most notable victories in 1979, was next, but Delp was already worrying about the weights. New Yorkers well remembered Laz Barrera's refusal to send Affirmed to face Bid the year before in the same race because of the weight spread (133 pounds to 124).

There was no equal to Bid among the 1980 three-year-old class, but several older horses were capable of beating any horse if they had favorable weight assignments.

New York racing secretary Lenny Hale studied the past performances of the Marlboro Cup nominees and decided to assign Spectacular Bid 136 pounds for the mile and one-eighth test. He gave Glorious Song 117 pounds off of her performance in the Haskell, a shift of

four pounds in her favor; the Belmont and Travers Stakes winner Temperence Hill received 119 (124 on the scale, which gives three-year-olds a five-pound concession at that time of year); and Suburban and Brooklyn Handicaps winner Winter's Tale, a brilliant but brittle gelding owned by Paul Mellon, was given 123 pounds.

Winter's Tale was a dangerous horse when fit, and Glorious Song had proved her mettle at Monmouth. Besides, 136 pounds was a lot of weight, even against lesser horses.

From Hale's standpoint, one could make the argument that Bid's races in California during the winter would have justified higher weights in subsequent races and that he had benefited from the conditions of those races that kept his weight assignments under restraint.

Publicly, the Spectacular Bid camp said little about the weights, hinting they didn't like them, but that they might run anyway. Privately, Delp had decided to skip the Marlboro and had released Shoemaker for the event.

Harry Meyerhoff says the weights were not the deciding factor: "If he'd had an easier race at Monmouth, we'd have thought seriously about the Marlboro, even at those weights."

When entries were taken on the Thursday before the September 6 Marlboro, Bid was not among them. Shortly afterward, Delp released a note criticizing Hale's weights and citing Affirmed's defection the year before because of the same problem.

The 136-pound assignment was high, but scarcely unprecedented. Delp took some pounding in the press for his lack of sportsmanship, with the usual hand wringing over how commercialism is now more important than the outcome of the contest, etc.

The majority opinion held that Bid should have run, and if not, Delp should have kept his mouth shut about Hale's weights, especially the references to the prior year.

Regardless, the race went on without Bid, and Winter's Tale was superior, beating Glorious Song by four and a half lengths in 1:47. Comparing the Haskell to the Marlboro is a dangerous thing to do. But Bid gave Glorious Song the equivalent of a fourteen-pound beating in the Haskell, and Winter's Tale beat her by about seven pounds, thus giving Bid a seven-pound or so advantage over Winter's Tale. Thus, Bid would likely have had difficulty giving Winter's Tale 13 pounds in the Marlboro, if one draws a straight line between the Haskell and the Marlboro.

In fact, that might well have been a fair reflection of the merits of the two horses, which the racing world was expecting to see played out on the racetrack in the Woodward Stakes on September 20.

Weights would not be a factor in the mile and a quarter Woodward, a weight-for-age race, which in its twenty-six previous editions had often had a bearing on the outcome of year-end championships.

Not many sane horsemen, or others for that matter, were interested in taking on Bid and Winter's Tale at weight for age, but the New York racing office hustled Temperence Hill and champion sprinter Dr. Patches, who had good form going longer, into entering.

Neither seemed terribly interested in running, with Temperence Hill's trainer Joe Cantey saying he would only consider running if one of the big two scratched.

Prior to this, Bid had worked five furlongs in :58 3/5 on the Tuesday before the Woodward, and Winter's Tale ripped through the same trip at Belmont the next morning in :57 4/5, neither work a comfort to the other horse's connections.

Friday morning brought a new and unfortunate twist to the proceedings. Trainer Mack Miller felt heat above Winter's Tale's left knee, had it X-rayed, and was told the gelding had a non-displaced (non-floating) chip on the radius, the bone above the knee. While the animal had shown no lameness, Miller talked with Mellon and decided to scratch the Marlboro victor from the Woodward and rest him.

That set in motion a chess match involving New York Racing Association officials and the three remaining horses' connections.

Cantey said he would talk to his owner, but he was reluctant to run in a race where his horse, who lacked early speed, would be at a disadvantage. Jan Nerud, conditioner of Dr. Patches, had not trained his horse for the race and also was disinclined to start.

Both talked with Lenny Hale and with NYRA chairman Ogden Mills "Dinny" Phipps and said they would run if the association wished them to do so. While the full story may never be known, it is clear that NYRA did not ask either to run, and there was speculation that both were encouraged to scratch rather than to have a race in name only with limited wagering.

NYRA, of course, also stood to save a lot of purse money if Temperence Hill and Dr. Patches stayed in

their respective stalls. Not only would second and third money be saved, but under New York racing law, as is typical elsewhere, a one-horse race is declared a walkover. The winner is entitled to half the guaranteed purse, plus the nomination fees, but not the entry money. Spectacular Bid would get $73,300 for an afternoon one and a quarter-mile workout.

Delp found out about the purse rule when NYRA vet Dr. Manny Gilman was making his Saturday morning rounds. Since walkovers are rare, occurring only in stakes races and very infrequently at that, Delp did not know the rule. When he told the Meyerhoffs, they were not pleased.

A discussion ensued, and they talked of not running the horse, but thought better of it after considering Hale's proffering that a $73,300 check for a workout was not a bad thing.

Harry Meyerhoff said later that the rule regarding walkovers stated the association "may" reduce the purse by half, not "must," and he believes some pay back was involved.

"The whole thing left a bad taste in our mouths. We thought they (the NYRA management) were pissed off because we didn't run in the Whitney."

The atmosphere around the Woodward was subdued, and the commentators for the national telecast were faced with the task of explaining how it ended up being a one-horse race and why Bid had to run at all.

The rules require horses that walkover to make an effort, and Bid's "workout" was a race-winning effort in most cases. Harry Meyerhoff, trying to lighten up an awkward situation, said he gave Shoemaker strict instructions: "Don't fall off." Entirely alone except for Shoemaker, Bid bowled along through easy fractions (six furlongs in 1:14 1/5, the mile in 1:38 1/5), then stepped it up down the lane, running the last quarter in :24 1/5 and finishing in 2:02 2/5.

His was the first walkover in a meaningful race since Coaltown's gallop around Havre de Grace in 1949 in the Edward Burke Handicap. Both Citation (1948) and Whirlaway (1942) walked over in Pimlico Specials, when their superiority and weight-for-age conditions caused everyone to avoid the entry box.

It was anti-climactic, but a tribute to the respect for Spectacular Bid among American horsemen that only Winter's Tale was willing to try him in the Woodward, and after his defection, there was nobody else.

The long-range plan for Bid's four-year-old season had always included a final race in the Jockey Club Gold Cup at Belmont on October 4. The Gold Cup at $500,000-added was the richest race in America at the time. It was also a race steeped in history, with many of its winners going on to Horse of the Year or other championship honors. Shortened in 1976 from two miles to one and a half miles, it was intended to be a year-end championship gathering place for the country's elite horses. It also was the race Bid had lost to Affirmed after a terrific struggle the year before.

Fresh from his non-race in the Woodward, Bid zipped six furlongs at Bowie in Maryland on Sunday, September 28, in 1:10 3/5, a tremendous workout, indicating that Delp was priming the colt for a spectacular farewell.

Bid shipped to New York on Tuesday, then galloped on Wednesday and Thursday, doing a bit more than Delp wanted him to that morning. On Friday, there was some filling in the left front ankle, and Dr. Harthill took X-rays.

Delp told the Meyerhoffs he thought the horse could still run, but the decision would not need to be made until after he galloped on Saturday morning.

That gallop took place without incident, and the horse appeared to be fine, but when Gilman showed up at the barn to perform his standard pre-race examination, the horse was standing in ice, and Harry Meyerhoff said he could not be taken from his stall.

Gilman returned an hour later, but found the horse being X-rayed again (the left fore) and his right leg bandaged with instruction from Delp, who was not at the track, that the bandages were not to be removed.

When Gilman came back a third time, he was told the bandages could come off, but that Bid was not to have his legs flexed or to be taken from his stall. This prevented Gilman from doing his normal checkup, and he reported this to the stewards, who informed NYRA management.

Adding to the delicacy of the matter was the discomfort between NYRA and Delp over the use of Harthill, whose presence was frowned upon in New York. NYRA security personnel escorted Harthill to and from the barn and kept him under a watchful eye as he examined and treated Bid.

Ultimately, Phipps and NYRA president Jim Heffernan drove to Bid's barn, where Delp arrived to

take the horse out of his stall and walk him. He seemed "off" in the left fore, and shortly afterward he was scratched from the Gold Cup.

X-rays had revealed two chips around the left inner sesamoid, one of which had been present for awhile, probably since the winter at Santa Anita. The other, new, possibly had been sustained that week. Harthill later said Bid stepped in a hole at Belmont on the Thursday before the Gold Cup and sprained the ankle, although he wasn't sure the sprain and the chips were related.

Harry Meyerhoff said they still would have considered running him, believing Bid to be well up to this final task, but Harthill advised against it, saying he could possibly break down.

"It was a very difficult decision," says Meyerhoff. "But, he was too valuable and had been too good to us to take a risk."

So, it was at the barn, not in the winner's circle, that Spectacular Bid's racing career ended. He would have an exhibition gallop on a Saturday night between races at the Meadowlands, sharing the stage with pacing superstar Niatross. The latter had earned much of his reputation as perhaps harness racing's best-ever pacer at the northern

New Jersey track, and Meadowlands management wanted to honor horse racing's latest two superstars as they were sent off to stud.

Afterward, Bid climbed on the van to go to his new home at Claiborne in Paris, Kentucky.

Life would return to normal at the Delp barn, but things would never be the same after the departure of the best horse Bud Delp had ever seen.

Although Bid's campaign in New York hardly went as hoped or planned, the magnitude of his achievements was etched alongside those of the best horses to race in North America.

His final tally:

| Starts | 1st | 2nd | 3rd | Earnings |
|--------|-----|-----|-----|----------|
| 30 | 26 | 2 | 1 | $2,781,608 |

The earnings total was a world record, and his twenty-six wins included twenty-three stakes races. He had been a champion of his class at the end of each of his three seasons and was named Horse of the Year in 1980.

His record that year of nine for nine, all major stakes races, could only be compared with the 1953 record of Tom Fool, who won all ten starts en route to Horse of the Year honors.

He literally did everything good horses are supposed to do — sprint, stay, carry weight, beat the best. He was the rarest of talents, according to Shoemaker, a horse capable of multiple moves in a single race.

Harry Meyerhoff believes Bid could have been champion sprinter at four had they chosen to run him in the Vosburgh at the Belmont fall meeting: "After his race in the Malibu, if he had won the Vosburgh I think they would have had to name him the champion sprinter. But with the other big races available, there was no point in it, or running on the grass, either."

Bid improved each year he raced and demonstrated impressive and relentless consistency. He did not have bad days, and when he was less than his best, he was still extremely good. The only horse to beat him on a day when he was the normal Bid was another great one, Affirmed, and it was easy to imagine the four-year-old Bid reversing that decision had the opportunity been presented.

He made everything around him better, taking the Meyerhoffs through racing experiences of a lifetime, allowing them to live a dream they could not have imagined, and earning Eclipse Awards for himself (four of them), Delp (leading trainer in 1980), and Franklin (leading apprentice rider of 1978).

For the Meyerhoffs, he was "the experience of a lifetime," says Harry Meyerhoff. "You never expect to have one like him, and you know you'll never get another one. It was euphoric — we felt like we were on top of the world. He was a major, major part of our lives for three years."

"Bud handled the horse wonderfully; I only wish he'd used Velcro wraps instead of bandages," he said tongue in cheek, referring to the safety-pin incident at the '79 Belmont.

Delp, in his own salute to Bid's owners, boycotted the Eclipse Awards dinner in 1981, even though he and Bid would be honored recipients, because he thought the Meyerhoffs should have been named the leading owners of 1980.

Others agreed, in part because the Meyerhoffs kept Bid in training at four despite paying insurance premiums in excess of his on-track earnings for the year.

This was a horse who changed lives and enriched lots of people. Most of all, the sight of his streaked visage repeatedly strolling away from the best horses of his generation left American racing fans certain that

they had seen a racehorse fully up to the standards of the icons of the sport, undoubtedly among the best ever to wear or peer through a bridle. He was fast, strong, sound, and managed superbly by a guy who, when given a chance, recognized and handled greatness with skill and refreshing audacity.

Spectacular Bid left the stage with a legion of admirers, carrying enormous respect and the well-wishes of horsemen who were glad they would not have to contend with him again.

# EPILOGUE

## *Better By Far On The Track*

T*he Blood-Horse* magazine cover of January 24, 1981, featured a photo of Spectacular Bid, led by Claiborne Farm veteran groom Clay Arnold, on his way to his paddock, walking past a familiar-looking chestnut named Secretariat.

There they were, two icons of the American racing scene of the 1970s, now far from adoring fans and the busy, sometimes high-tension environment of the racetrack, engaged in the business of foal production.

It is important to note the use of the term "business," because the period when Spectacular Bid entered stud was remarkable in the history of Thoroughbred breeding.

From the end of World War II to the mid-1970s, the trends in the Thoroughbred marketplace — as measured by yearling prices, stallion values, and foal production — had shown a steady, relatively uninterrupted, upward bias. Foal production had, for example, increased from 9,095 in 1950 to 35,679 by 1980, and yearling averages went from $2,944 ($5,056,394 in total sales) to $29,683 ($210,128,000 in total sales) over the same time frame.

Stallion syndication, a post-war development that gave breeders greater access to the top sire prospects than ever before, also spread risk and allowed prices for both new and proven sires to rise as high as the market would bear. By 1981, that was very high indeed.

The emergence of the international marketplace — driven by the success of American-bred horses in Europe from the late 1960s onward and the emergence of Asian, mostly Japanese, buyers as a formidable force, followed by an avalanche of Middle East petrol dollars — brought a tidal wave of new money into the American markets that not only would drive a phenomenal bull market in yearling prices, stud fees, and broodmare values, but would actually lead to a change in pedigree fashion.

Oddly, the photo of Bid and Secretariat on *The Blood-Horse* cover in early 1981 would represent the twilight of the old order, at least in terms of stallion fashion.

The dominance of the Phalaris male line, emanating from the high-quality but scarcely memorable English sprinter-miler of the 1920s, was by that time widely acknowledged, but a major shift in its dominant branches was about to occur.

As noted earlier, Nasrullah and his sons, especially Bid's paternal grandsire, Bold Ruler, had swept to the fore in the 1950s and were North America's strongest influence for both speed and middle-distance class for about twenty-five years or so. In fact, the aforementioned dominance of the American classics by Bold Ruler-line horses in the '70s, beginning with Secretariat, was so pronounced that it would have taken a brave soul to predict a collapse even more sudden than its ascent.

While no son of Bold Ruler had emerged as a consistent force at the top of the stallion ranks, and perhaps this was a tell-tale indicator, enough of them had sired major stakes winners and championship-caliber horses, such as Bid, to suggest that the next great sire or sires from this male line was soon to emerge.

The breeding industry, however, is an ever-shifting mosaic, and the new darlings of the stallion ranks were Northern Dancer and Raise a Native, and their many sons.

128

Northern Dancer had, of course, established his racing merit with wins in the 1964 Kentucky Derby and Preakness, while Raise a Native had flashed superior form in an all-too-brief four-race career as a juvenile in 1963. Both had sire credentials sufficient to guarantee solid patronage, but both had potential debits to overcome.

Northern Dancer was small, if well-made, and a son of Nearctic, a useful, but by no means eye-catching, sprinter. Although a son of the great Nearco, who also sired Nasrullah and Royal Charger, Nearctic was not fashionable, and particularly not to the private breeders who sought to breed classic types or to market breeders attempting to get the best blend of racing performance and pedigree.

Northern Dancer, though, would establish early that his genetic makeup, and his ability to pass on that makeup, was a composite of the best elements of his pedigree. After his son Nijinsky II appeared in Northern Dancer's second crop to become England's first Triple Crown winner in thirty-five years, the doughty little son of Nearctic became the gatekeeper to a European invasion of American bloodstock markets.

Even if most of the best Northern Dancers raced in

Europe, and many of his best-bred yearlings were automatically ticketed to head across the Atlantic, he symbolized the emergence of the American Thoroughbred as the best in the world. By the early '80s, Northern Dancer had become indisputably the world's most glamorous stallion, and he had earned that place.

Raise a Native, as unsound as he was fast, often sired horses with size, soft ankles, or open knees in about equal measure, but they could still run, enough so to make him the great speed sire of his time.

The best of Raise a Native was epitomized by the talents of son Majestic Prince, who would sire Bid's nemesis Coastal; grandson Affirmed, the relentless warrior of the 1978 Triple Crown; and son Alydar, pursuer of Affirmed and a great middle-distance star himself.

Yet, it would not be those horses, all of classic caliber, who would carry the banner of the Raise a Native line; instead, that honor would fall, fittingly, to a more prototypical son of Raise a Native, the ubiquitous Mr. Prospector.

The latter was a sprinter with persistent soundness problems who never demonstrated the ability to beat good horses around two turns. He went to Florida to begin a stud career that it was hoped would see him at least be an influence for speed.

By the time Bid reached Claiborne, it was clear Mr. Prospector was not only a superior sire, but also one with several dimensions.

Mr. Prospector's move to Claiborne in 1981, along with the arrival of a lightly raced son of Northern Dancer named Danzig, would be the stimulus for Claiborne's continued role as a vital source of sire power in America, but with a change of focus. The Nasrullah-Bold Ruler line would fade, despite the presence at Claiborne of two of its finest race-course standard-bearers, Secretariat and Spectacular Bid.

Secretariat had four crops on the racetrack when Bid joined him at Claiborne, with a fifth ready to step forth. To the regret of his millions of admirers, it had become evident that Secretariat, while not a failure at stud, was not going to emulate either his sire, Bold Ruler, or his half-brother, the successful stallion Sir Gaylord.

A few quality Secretariats had made their marks, such as General Assembly and the brilliantly fast filly Terlingua, and more would come (Lady's Secret, Risen Star, among others), but he was not consistently siring the volume of quality offspring expected, or at least hoped for.

Bid, if one evaluated his prospects coldly, perhaps stood less of a chance of making it than his illustrious barnmate.

His own sire, Bold Bidder, could be termed successful, but not remarkably so, having gotten good racehorses in fair quantity but not a son or sons that were exceptional at stud. Bid's female family was essentially bereft of sire talent, not a matter of comfort to breeders being asked to pay the high stud fees ($150,000 in Bid's case) for horses of Bid's racing class. His pedigree also contained more stamina than speed elements, especially among its more prominent members.

Even among the sires scattered through the internal parts of his pedigree, one had to go back three or four generations to find horses of lasting impact on the breed.

Seth Hancock, who had cut his syndication teeth with Secretariat and Riva Ridge in 1973, recalls Ogden Phipps, a long-time Claiborne client and adviser, saying of Spectacular Bid, "He doesn't have any pedigree." Hancock responded, "Mr. Phipps, there have been three great racehorses in a row in this country — Seattle Slew, Affirmed, and Spectacular Bid — and none of them have had much pedigree. One of them is going to make a helluva sire." He was right, but that one would be Seattle Slew.

What Bid had going for him was a race record to kill for, a well-earned reputation as one of the most capable and consistent horses to race in America in decades, well worthy of comparison to the best of his '70s contemporaries — Secretariat, Forego, Affirmed, Seattle Slew — and to the great horses that preceded them.

He was the quintessential modern racehorse: a maven of middle distances able to produce devastating acceleration at any time, often more than once during a race. Interestingly though, for a horse possessed of such great speed, he was very tractable, not the pillar-to-post type of, say, Seattle Slew vintage.

With the fashion shifting to the Northern Dancers and Raise a Natives, would greatness on the racetrack be enough to assure him the types of mares to make him an important stallion? Hancock said, "He (Bid) was brilliant at two, three, and four, and he was sound. I thought he'd get sound, tough, hard-knocking horses."

Bid's first book of mares in 1981 was, on paper, a quality group, including Buckpasser mares Lassie Dear and Swingtime, the classy In Reality mare Me and

Connie, the Damascus mare Regal Rumor, the crack race mare Water Malone (by Naskra), Fairway Fable (by Never Bend), Continuation (by Forli), and Haitien and State (both by Nijinsky II). The book was full of black-type earners and producers, and the result was twenty-five named foals.

Hancock recalls the first foals "didn't knock our eyes out, but there was nothing wrong with them, either, and the ones that went to auction sold well."

Of those, twelve got to the races as two-year-olds, and one, the colt Spectacular Love, won the grade I Futurity Stakes at Belmont and was third in the grade II Hollywood Juvenile Championship Stakes.

There would be no champions or near-champions among the first Bids to race, but seven stakes winners came from that first crop, a spectacular twenty-eight percent from named foals. There was, however, only one other graded-stakes winner in the crop, the filly Spectacular Joke, who started her career in Europe and won the group II Prix Maurice de Gheest and group III Prix du Palais Royal as a three-year-old.

Of the six members of Bid's first crop to go abroad to race, three were stakes winners or stakes-placed,

including the Me and Connie colt Spectame, a solid miler in France. Among other things, this suggested his progeny might do well on grass, a surface he had never tried except when grazing, although Delp had talked about closing out his three- and four-year-old seasons in Laurel Park's Washington, D.C., International.

On the whole, though, his first crop was a mixed bag. They did not last terribly long, and there were only sporadic bursts of exceptional class. Still, the number of black-type earners was encouraging, and no one was yet suggesting that Bid was going to join the list of great racehorses that fail as stallions.

His next crop, foals of 1983, was much larger (fifty-one named foals) and the mare selection was even more impressive than his first book, including Arachne (by Intentionally), Swift Response (Dr. Fager), Alma North (Northern Dancer), The Very One (One For All), Fashionable Trick (Buckpasser), Old Goat (Olden Times), Glowing Tribute (Graustark), Gay Meeting (Sir Gaylord), and repeat visitors Continuation, Me and Connie, Regal Rumor, and State. In fact, this list could easily be augmented by another equally impressive roster from the same book of mares.

The results: five stakes winners, several solid allowance horses, and a host of lightly raced winners. Notably, none of his stakes winners earned black type as two-year-olds and the crop's record at two was distinguished by a scarcity of starts and wins beyond maiden levels.

Also, the five stakes winners included four fillies, a reversal from the first crop, where five males and two females won stakes. The best of this group was Double Feint, out of State, a gray colt who won twice at two, then earned his first stakes credentials at three. He won eleven of thirty career starts, including the grade III Hill Prince Stakes and the Poker Stakes at Belmont Park. He also finished fourth in the 1986 Breeders' Cup Mile on Santa Anita's grass course.

Double Feint was competitive on dirt but better on turf, as was the filly Festivity, the other major stakes winner in the '83 crop. She captured the grade II Palomar Handicap at Del Mar and was second or third in four other graded stakes on grass.

The best dirt horse in the bunch was Ann's Bid, who won four stakes and earned $310,733 in a thirty-three-race career spanning four seasons.

The third crop is often critical for any sire, because the

first two crops have been scrutinized at the yearling sales and the early whispers on two-year-olds are being heard. Bid's third crop consisted of fifty named foals from a book that, in qualitative terms, matched his first two.

Statistically, it would be his best, with eight stakes winners among them. Probably the best was Lay Down, a gelding out of the Majestic Prince mare Impish. Lay Down had some physical problems and didn't get to the races until he was three. He then won graded stakes in each of the next three seasons, among them the Forego Handicap at Saratoga, Excelsior Handicap at Aqueduct, and Washington Park Handicap at Arlington Park, all grade II events.

He ended his career eleven for twenty-nine, earning $593,423 and respect as a versatile, solid performer. He was, in essence, a prototype of the good Spectacular Bids, consistent and capable of winning in good company but something less than top drawer.

His competition as best in class was Legal Bid, a son of the quality Boldnesian mare Bold Bikini. Legal Bid did his racing in England, and he was a strong performer over classic distances, winning the group III Highland Spring Derby Trial at Lingfield and the

Feilden Stakes at Newmarket, which prompted him to be cast as third choice in the 1987 Epsom Derby, where he could only finish fourteenth.

He rebounded to finish a good second in the group II King Edward VII Stakes at Royal Ascot and had subsequent seconds in two other route races. Overall, he won three times and was second three times in seven career starts, earning a Timeform rating of 120, making him what he was, an able performer some seven or eight pounds below average classic form.

Five of the eight stakes winners from this crop were fillies, and six of them won stakes on the grass, including the good fillies Sum (three stakes wins, $197,578 in earnings) and Spectacular Bev (two stakes wins, $167,257).

By the time these horses were establishing their form, the verdict on Bid as a commercial proposition was in: His first foals sold as yearlings in 1983 for an average of $708,182. By 1986, they averaged $141,000, and although the market was in the early stages of a major decline, the market for Spectacular Bid's offspring was in freefall.

He wasn't reproducing himself in type, much less in talent, and that is usually a bad sign to erstwhile buyers and breeders, for it suggests a stallion being dominated by his mares and their genetic pool.

Even though he had eight stakes winners in his next crop, none was exceptional, and the trend was now firmly in place. Here was a horse who had gotten high-quality books from the beginning and was still attracting good mares. He could not be termed an abject failure, but certainly a major disappointment.

Clearly, Bid's genetic contribution was not equal to the quality of the mares bred to him, and there was no hint of any of his sons or daughters approaching him in terms of ability.

Hancock says that, in hindsight, with twenty additional years of observing stallions, he probably wouldn't have syndicated the horse today because, "I've learned that pedigree really does matter; it's a rare horse who can overcome a weak pedigree and even when one does, you can usually look back and see that their pedigree got hot later."

Evaluating the other glamour-boy horses of the '70s — Secretariat, Seattle Slew, Affirmed, Alydar, and Spectacular Bid — the best stallions, now that a longer perspective is available, are Seattle Slew and Alydar. A major part of that success lay in the fact that both were able to sire the classic or major-race winner on a regular basis. Of the two, Seattle Slew is the one who appears to have established an ongoing male line.

Secretariat sired a few exceptional horses, the best being champions Risen Star and Lady's Secret, but his overall record was moderate, and his sons have done little, although he is a first-rate broodmare sire. Affirmed was consistent, but did not sire the "big" horse, nor are his sons doing much to perpetuate him.

After the 1986 foal crop, the quality of Bid's books, although not terrible, was in decline, and it was a 1987 foal, Lotus Pool, out of the Mr. Prospector mare Golden Petal, who would become his leading earner and a world traveler. Lotus Pool began his career in Ireland, where he was a stakes winner and third in the group I Irish Two Thousand Guineas.

Returning home at four, he was a respectable runner, then became a top competitor at five, when he won three grass stakes and was second or third in four others. Over his career, Lotus Pool won or placed in thirteen stakes and earned $694,543. He was a durable and capable turf horse.

In that same crop was the good grass filly Starfield, who won three stakes, two on grass, and was second or third in four others on her way to $278,297 in earnings.

After that, the stakes winners were far less frequent, a direct function of the loss of confidence by breeders. Spectacular Bid was no longer a serious commercial proposition, and his broodmare book reflected that, declining steadily in quality and numbers. He was now a second-tier stallion at Claiborne, and in late 1991 he was no longer that, being moved to Milfer Farm in upstate New York, about a two-hour drive west of Saratoga, where he would stand for a $15,000 stud fee.

Hancock says Harry Meyerhoff approached him, almost tearfully, at the Keeneland September sale that year about an offer to move him to New York.

"The Meyerhoffs were always great to deal with, always up front. When Harry mentioned moving the horse, I said, 'Harry, I want to do what's best for Spectacular Bid and moving him to New York is probably best for him. He's dead in the water here and things aren't going to get better.' "

Upstate New York is peaceful, timeless country, gently rolling and heavily forested, not remarkably different from its state of 300 years ago, when it was the heartland of the Iroquois nation. Milfer occupies about 2,000 acres, and Bid is the farm's elder statesman, a legend living out a good life in the quiet of the north woods. He is still active as a sire, with foal crops in the mid-teens and a book of pleasure horse mares, besides.

There is an occasional good one — the 1994 filly Princess Pietrina, who earned $406,639 from 1996 to 1999, and Marquette, a 1996 colt who can run when he can get to the track ($255,442 in earnings, four wins in ten starts, including the grade II National Museum of Racing Hall of Fame Handicap at Saratoga) — but no one seriously expects a belated Bid suddenly to set the world on fire and give us a final glimpse of the greatness that was the sire.

Spectacular Bid's stud career has been, if not a disaster, certainly a large disappointment given the quality of his Claiborne books. His forty-four stakes winners and overall percentages of starters and winners are not bad, just not what was expected. While one can only speculate as to the reasons great racehorses frequently do not reproduce themselves, it must be said that Bid's female family lacked sire quality, nor were there many stallions in his five-generation pedigree that established lasting male-line influences.

While this might be regarded as hindsight evaluation, Bid's stud career provides compelling evidence that, as Seth Hancock said, in breeding matters, pedigree — the entire pedigree — does count.

Now sporting a granite-hued coat, Bid still moves with a grace that makes him seem younger than his twenty-four years, spending his final years in quiet dignity.

If his legacy is not to be found in future pedigrees, it will be forever recalled in the repositories of racing history and in the minds of those who remember his race-course power and dominance. His record and reputation were built, not on glamour or hype — his trainer notwithstanding — but on the towering achievements of a race career rarely equaled.

Along the way, he gave Bud Delp, the Meyerhoffs, Ron Franklin, Jorge Velasquez, Bill Shoemaker, and thousands of fans a great ride.

Best horse to ever look through a bridle? The fact that such a comment was even a matter of debate makes the ultimate statement about his greatness.

# SPECTACULAR BID's
## PEDIGREE

| | | Nasrullah, 1940 | Nearco<br>Mumtaz Begum |
|---|---|---|---|
| | Bold Ruler, 1954 | | |
| | | Miss Disco, 1944 | Discovery<br>Outdone |
| BOLD BIDDER,<br>b, 1962 | | | |
| | | **To Market, 1948** | **Market Wise<br>Pretty Does** |
| | High Bid, 1956 | | |
| SPECTACULAR BID,<br>gray colt,<br>1976 | | Stepping Stone, 1950 | Princequillo<br>Step Across |
| | | Palestinian, 1946 | Sun Again<br>Dolly Whisk |
| | Promised Land, 1954 | | |
| | | Mahmoudess, 1942 | Mahmoud<br>Forever Yours |
| SPECTACULAR,<br>ro, 1970 | | | |
| | | **To Market, 1948** | **Market Wise<br>Pretty Does** |
| | Stop On Red, 1959 | | |
| | | Danger Ahead, 1946 | Hard Play<br>Lady Beware |

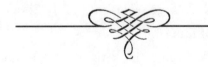

# SPECTACULAR BID's RACE RECORD

**Spectacular Bid** — **gr. c. 1976, by Bold Bidder (Bold Ruler)–Spectacular, by Promised Land** — **Lifetime record: 30 26 2 1 $2,781,608**

**Own.– Hawksworth Farm**
**Br.– Mmes Gilmour & Jason (Ky)**
**Tr.– Grover G. Delp**

| | | | | | | | | | | | | | | | | | | |
|---|---|---|---|---|---|---|---|---|---|---|---|---|---|---|---|---|---|---|
| 20Sep80- 0Bel | fst | 1¼ | :50$^{2}$ 1:14$^{1}$ 1:38$^{1}$ 2:02$^{2}$ | 3↑ Woodward-G1 | 1 | 1 | 1 | 1 | 1 | 1 | Shoemaker W | 126 | | 88-21 | Spectacular Bid126 | In hand | 1 |
| | Walkover,run between 7th and 8th race - Walkover,no wagering | | | | | | | | | | | | | | | | |
| 16Aug80- 9Mth | fst | 1⅛ | :46$^{4}$ 1:11$^{1}$ 1:35$^{3}$ 1:48 | 3↑ AL Haskell H-G1 | 5 | 7 | 65½ | 5¾ | 1½ | 11¾ | Shoemaker W | 132 | *.10 | 95-15 | SpectcularBd132$^{1\frac{3}{4}}$Glorious Song117$^{1\frac{1}{4}}$The Cool Virginian112$^{4}$ | | 8 |
| | Ridden out | | | | | | | | | | | | | | | | |
| 19Jly80- 8AP | fst | 1⅛ | :46$^{1}$ 1:09$^{4}$ 1:34 1:46$^{1}$ | 3↑ Wash Park-G3 | 4 | 4 | 44 | 2hd | 14 | 110 | Shoemaker W | 130 | *.05 | 103-17 | SpectacularBid130$^{10}$HoldYourTrcks119$^{8}$Archtct119$^{1\frac{1}{2}}$ | Easily | 6 |
| 8Jun80- 8Hol | fst | 1⅛ | :45 1:08$^{4}$ 1:33$^{1}$ 1:45$^{4}$ | 3↑ Californian-G1 | 3 | 3 | 31½ | 11 | 16 | 14¼ | Shoemaker W | 130 | *.05 | 103-05 | SpectaculrBid130$^{4\frac{1}{4}}$PaintKng115$^{3\frac{3}{4}}$CroBmbno118$^{8}$ | Easy score | 7 |
| 18May80- 8Hol | fst | 1$\frac{1}{16}$ | :22$^{3}$ :45$^{2}$ 1:08$^{4}$ 1:40$^{2}$ | 3↑ Mervyn LeRoy H-G2 | 1 | 5 | 42 | 2hd | 13½ | 17 | Shoemaker W | 132 | *.20 | 93-18 | SpectaculrBd132$^{7}$Peregrintor119$^{\frac{3}{4}}$Beau'sEgl121$^{2}$ | Ridden out | 6 |
| 2Mar80- 8SA | sly | 1¼ | :48$^{3}$ 1:12$^{2}$ 1:36$^{4}$ 2:00$^{3}$ | 4↑ S Anita H-G1 | 5 | 2 | 22½ | 1hd | 12½ | 15 | Shoemaker W | 130 | *.30 | 90-18 | SpctaclarBid130$^{5}$FlyingPstr123$^{8}$Beau'sEgl122$^{14}$ | Ridden out | 5 |
| 3Feb80- 8SA | fst | 1¼ | :44$^{3}$ 1:08$^{2}$ 1:32$^{4}$ 1:57$^{4}$ | C H Strub-G1 | 3 | 4 | 29 | 2hd | 13 | 13¼ | Shoemaker W | 126 | *.30 | 104-08 | SpectacularBid126$^{3\frac{1}{4}}$FlyingPaster121$^{9}$Vldz122$^{\frac{1}{2}}$ | Handy score | 4 |
| 19Jan80- 8SA | gd | 1⅛ | :46$^{2}$ 1:11 1:35$^{3}$ 1:48 | San Fernando-G2 | 1 | 3 | 33½ | 1hd | 1½ | 11½ | Shoemaker W | 126 | *.05 | 89-19 | SpectacularBid126$^{1\frac{1}{2}}$FlyngPstr126$^{15}$Rlunch120$^{33}$ | Drew clear | 4 |
| 5Jan80- 8SA | fst | 7f | :22$^{1}$ :44$^{2}$ 1:08 1:20 | Malibu-G2 | 3 | 4 | 52½ | 41 | 1½ | 15 | Shoemaker W | 126 | *.30 | 103-10 | SpectacularBid126$^{5}$FlyingPastr123$^{1\frac{1}{2}}$Ros'sSvll117$^{no}$ | Easily | 5 |
| 18Oct79- 6Med | fst | 1¼ | :47$^{4}$ 1:12 1:36$^{2}$ 2:01$^{1}$ | 3↑ Med Cup H-G2 | 1 | 3 | 33 | 1½ | 11½ | 13 | Shoemaker W | 126 | *.10 | 102-14 | Spectacular Bid126$^{3}$Smarten120$^{hd}$Valdez121$^{11}$ | Drew out | 5 |
| 6Oct79- 8Bel | fst | 1½ | :49 1:13$^{1}$ 2:02$^{2}$ 2:27$^{2}$ | 3↑ J C Gold Cup-G1 | 2 | 3 | 2½ | 31 | 2½ | 2¾ | Shoemaker W | 121 | 1.40 | 82-21 | Affirmed126$^{\frac{3}{4}}$Spectacular Bid121$^{3}$Coastal121$^{31}$ | Gamely | 4 |
| 8Sep79- 8Bel | fst | 1⅛ | :47$^{2}$ 1:11 1:34$^{1}$ 1:46$^{3}$ | 3↑ Marlboro Cup H-G1 | 5 | 3 | 1hd | 1½ | 13 | 15 | Shoemaker W | 124 | *.50 | 94-17 | SpectacularBid124$^{5}$GenrlAssmbly120$^{1\frac{1}{4}}$Costl122$^{\frac{1}{2}}$ | Ridden out | 6 |
| 26Aug79- 7Del | gd | 1$\frac{1}{16}$ | :23 :46$^{3}$ 1:11$^{1}$ 1:41$^{3}$ | Alw 18000 | 3 | 3 | 21½ | 16 | 112 | 117 | Shoemaker W | 122 | *.05 | 101-14 | SpectacularBd122$^{17}$ArmadaStrik112$^{7}$NotSoProud112$^{6}$ | Easily | 5 |
| 9Jun79- 8Bel | fst | 1½ | :47$^{3}$ 1:11$^{1}$ 2:02$^{2}$ 2:28$^{3}$ | Belmont-G1 | 3 | 2 | 2½ | 13 | 2½ | 33½ | Franklin RJ | 126 | *.30 | 73-17 | Coastal126$^{3\frac{1}{4}}$Golden Act126$^{nk}$Spectacular Bid126$^{9\frac{1}{2}}$ | Tired | 8 |
| 19May79- 8Pim | gd | 1$\frac{3}{16}$ | :46$^{4}$ 1:10$^{3}$ 1:35 1:54$^{1}$ | Preakness-G1 | 2 | 4 | 45 | 1hd | 16 | 15½ | Franklin RJ | 126 | *.10 | 99-09 | SpctacularBd126$^{5\frac{1}{2}}$GoldenAct126$^{4}$ScrnKng126$^{1\frac{1}{2}}$ | Ridden out | 5 |
| 5May79- 8CD | fst | 1¼ | :47$^{2}$ 1:12$^{2}$ 1:37$^{3}$ 2:02$^{2}$ | Ky Derby-G1 | 3 | 7 | 610 | 2hd | 11½ | 12¾ | Franklin RJ | 126 | *.60 | 85-14 | SpectacularBid126$^{2\frac{3}{4}}$GnrlAssmbly126$^{3}$GoldnAct126$^{1\frac{3}{4}}$ | Driving | 10 |
| 26Apr79- 7Kee | fst | 1⅛ | :46$^{3}$ 1:10$^{3}$ 1:36$^{1}$ 1:50 | Blue Grass-G1 | 4 | 4 | 1hd | 12 | 15½ | 17 | Franklin RJ | 121 | *.05 | 87-20 | Spectacular Bid121$^{7}$Lot o' Gold121$^{8}$Bishop's Choice121$^{10}$ | | 4 |
| | Easily best | | | | | | | | | | | | | | | | |
| 24Mar79-10Hia | fst | 1⅛ | :46 1:09$^{3}$ 1:35$^{1}$ 1:48$^{2}$ | Flamingo-G1 | 8 | 3 | 1½ | 18 | 110 | 112 | Franklin RJ | 122 | *.05 | 90-16 | Spectacular Bid122$^{12}$Strike the Min118$^{3}$Sir Ivor Again122$^{hd}$ | | 8 |
| | Ridden out | | | | | | | | | | | | | | | | |
| 6Mar79-11GP | fst | 1⅛ | :47$^{4}$ 1:11$^{4}$ 1:36$^{3}$ 1:48$^{4}$ | Florida Derby-G1 | 5 | 5 | 47½ | 3½ | 11½ | 14½ | Franklin RJ | 122 | *.05 | 90-14 | Spectacular Bid122$^{4\frac{1}{2}}$Lot o' Gold122$^{\frac{3}{4}}$Fantasy 'n Reality122$^{3}$ | | 7 |
| | Four wide,clear | | | | | | | | | | | | | | | | |
| 19Feb79- 9GP | fst | 1$\frac{1}{16}$ | :24 :47$^{2}$ 1:10$^{4}$ 1:41$^{1}$ | Fountain of Youth-G3 | 2 | 3 | 1hd | 13 | 14 | 18½ | Franklin RJ | 122 | *.10 | 95-12 | Spectacular Bid122$^{8\frac{1}{2}}$Lot o'Gold117$^{1}$Bishop's Choice122$^{1}$ | | 6 |
| | Ridden out | | | | | | | | | | | | | | | | |

## *SPECTACULAR BID's* **RACE RECORD** *CONTINUED*

| | | | | | | | | | | | | | | | | | | |
|---|---|---|---|---|---|---|---|---|---|---|---|---|---|---|---|---|---|---|
| 7Feb79- 9GP | fst 7f | :22$^4$ | :44$^4$ | 1:08$^4$ | 1:21$^2$ | Hutcheson 28k | 1 | 2 | 2$^{hd}$ | 2$^2$ | 1$^3$ | 1$^{3\frac{3}{4}}$ | Franklin RJ | 122 | *.05 | 97-22 | SpectcularBid122$^{3\frac{3}{4}}$Lot o' Gold114$^{7\frac{1}{2}}$Northern Prospect114$^{3\frac{1}{2}}$ | 4 |
| | In hand | | | | | | | | | | | | | | | | | |
| 11Nov78- 8Key | fst $1\frac{1}{16}$ | :22$^4$ | :46$^2$ | 1:10$^3$ | 1:42 | Heritage-G2 | 6 | 5 | 5$^5$ | 1$^{hd}$ | 1$^3$ | 1$^6$ | Franklin RJ | 122 | *.10 | 94-13 | SpctacularBid122$^6$SunWatcher112$^{3\frac{1}{4}}$TerrfcSon117$^{no}$ Handily | 7 |
| 28Oct78- 8Lrl | fst $1\frac{1}{16}$ | :23$^4$ | :46$^4$ | 1:11 | 1:41$^3$ | Lrl Futurity-G1 | 2 | 1 | 1$^{1\frac{1}{2}}$ | 1$^{\frac{1}{2}}$ | 1$^4$ | 1$^{8\frac{1}{2}}$ | Franklin RJ | 122 | *.90 | 105-14 | SpectacularBd122$^{8\frac{1}{2}}$General Assembly122$^{12}$Clever Trick122$^{3\frac{1}{2}}$ | 4 |
| | Driving | | | | | | | | | | | | | | | | | |
| 19Oct78- 6Med | fst $1\frac{1}{16}$ | :23$^2$ | :46$^2$ | 1:11$^1$ | 1:43$^1$ | Young America-G1 | 5 | 3 | 2$^{hd}$ | 2$^{\frac{1}{2}}$ | 2$^{hd}$ | 1$^{nk}$ | Velasquez J | 122 | *.30 | 95-14 | SpectclrBid122$^{nk}$StrikeYourColrs119$^{hd}$InstrumntLanding113$^4$ | 9 |
| | Driving | | | | | | | | | | | | | | | | | |
| 8Oct78- 8Bel | fst 1 | :23$^1$ | :46 | 1:10$^1$ | 1:34$^4$ | Champagne-G1 | 1 | 2 | 1$^1$ | 1$^{2\frac{1}{2}}$ | 1$^4$ | 1$^{2\frac{3}{4}}$ | Velasquez J | 122 | 2.40 | 94-19 | SpectclrBid122$^{2\frac{3}{4}}$GeneralAssembly122$^{5\frac{1}{2}}$Crest of theWave122$^{\frac{3}{4}}$ | 6 |
| | Ridden out | | | | | | | | | | | | | | | | | |
| 23Sep78- 8Atl | gd 7f | :22 | :44$^3$ | 1:09 | 1:20$^4$ | World's Playground-G3 | 3 | 3 | 1$^{\frac{1}{2}}$ | 1$^2$ | 1$^6$ | 1$^{15}$ | Franklin RJ | 114 | 5.20 | 98-25 | SpctaculrBid114$^{15}$CrstofthWv124$^{1\frac{1}{4}}$GrotonHgh118$^{\frac{1}{2}}$ Driving | 7 |
| 20Aug78- 9Del | fst 6f | :22$^2$ | :46 | :58 | 1:10$^4$ | Dover 34k | 2 | 4 | 4$^3$ | 5$^{3\frac{3}{4}}$ | 4$^4$ | 2$^{2\frac{1}{2}}$ | Franklin RJ | 112 | *1.00 | 88-13 | StrikeYourColors112$^{2\frac{1}{2}}$SpectacularBid112$^{5\frac{1}{2}}$Spy Charger122$^1$ | 7 |
| | 2nd best | | | | | | | | | | | | | | | | | |
| 2Aug78- 8Mth | sly $5\frac{1}{2}$f | :22$^4$ | :46$^1$ | :59 | 1:04$^4$ | Tyro (Div 2) 27k | 6 | 8 | 8$^{16}$ | 8$^{12}$ | 6$^{10}$ | 4$^{6\frac{3}{4}}$ | Franklin RJ | 118 | *1.70 | 86-22 | GrotonHigh122$^{2\frac{1}{2}}$GreatBoon116$^{nk}$OurGry116$^4$ Very wide early | 8 |
| 22Jly78- 5Pim | fst $5\frac{1}{2}$f | :22$^3$ | :46$^1$ | :58$^1$ | 1:04$^1$ | Alw 6500 | 3 | 4 | 3$^1$ | 1$^{hd}$ | 1$^3$ | 1$^8$ | Franklin RJ$^5$ | 115 | *.30 | 100-17 | SpectacularBid115$^8$SilentNative120$^9$DoublePrd114$^1$ Driving | 5 |
| 30Jun78- 3Pim | fst $5\frac{1}{2}$f | :22$^3$ | :46$^3$ | :58$^2$ | 1:04$^3$ | Md Sp Wt | 5 | 4 | 1$^{\frac{1}{2}}$ | 1$^{1\frac{1}{2}}$ | 1$^{2\frac{1}{2}}$ | 1$^{3\frac{1}{4}}$ | Franklin RJ$^5$ | 115 | 6.30 | 98-15 | Spectacular Bid115$^{3\frac{1}{4}}$Strike Your Colors120$^4$Instant Love112$^4$ | 11 |
| | Drew out | | | | | | | | | | | | | | | | | |

# *Index*

# Photo Credits

*Cover photo*: (Milt Toby)

*Page 1:* Spectacular Bid winning "The Bold Bidder" allowance (The Blood-Horse); Bid head shot (Milt Toby)

*Page 2:* Bid as a yearling (The Blood-Horse); Mrs. William Jason and Mrs. William Gilmore (The Blood-Horse)

*Page 3:* Bold Ruler (Allen F. Brewer Jr.); Bold Bidder (Turfotos); Promised Land (Bert and Richard Morgan); Spectacular (Milt Toby)

*Page 4-5:* Bud Delp (Milt Toby); Ron Franklin aboard Bid (Milt Toby); Bill Shoemaker (New York Racing Association photo); Meyerhoff Family in Derby winner's circle (Milt Toby); Herman Hall (Milt Toby)

*Page 6:* Bid winning World's Playground (Turfotos); Winning the Champagne (Bob Coglianese); Winning the Young America (Turfotos)

*Page 7:* Bid winning the Laurel Futurity (The Blood-Horse); Winning the Heritage Stakes (The Blood-Horse)

*Page 8:* Bid winning the Hutcheson (Turfotos); Winning the Flamingo (Turfotos); Winning the Florida Derby (Turfotos)

*Page 9:* Bid arriving in Lexington (The Blood-Horse); Winning the Blue Grass (Milt Toby)

*Page 10-11:* Bid in Kentucky Derby post parade (Milt Toby); Bid winning the Derby (Skip Ball); Winning the Preakness (The Blood-Horse); After the Preakness (The Blood-Horse); The Belmont finish (Bob Coglianese)

*Page 12:* Bid winning the Marlboro Cup (NYRA photo); Bid in his stall (Turfotos); Winning the Meadowlands Cup (Turfotos)

*Page 13:* Bid winning the Californian (Kevin Ellsworth); Winning the Santa Anita Handicap (The Blood-Horse); Winning the San Fernando Stakes (Vic Stein)

*Page 14:* Bid winning the Washington Park Stakes (The Blood-Horse); Winning the Amory L. Haskell (Turfotos)

*Page 15:* Bid at start of his Woodward walkover (Bob Coglianese); At the finish (The Blood-Horse); In the winner's circle (Bob Coglianese)

*Page 16:* Spectacular Love (Bob Coglianese); Double Feint (Four Footed Foto); Spectacular Bid at Milfer Farm (Barbara D. Livingston)

## ABOUT THE
# AUTHOR

T imothy T. Capps has been involved in nearly every aspect of the Thoroughbred industry. During the 1970s and mid-80s, Capps served as editor of *The Thoroughbred Record*, a leading industry monthly. In the mid-80s, he ventured into the high-stakes stallion market as an executive with Matchmaker, a company that sold stallion seasons and shares. From there, he was lured to the racetrack and went to Pimlico and Laurel Park in Maryland as a vice president. Today, Capps heads the Maryland Horse Breeders Association and oversees the Maryland Million, a championship event for Maryland racehorses. He also is editor and publisher of *MidAtlantic Thoroughbred*.

He has seen many of the great racehorses of the last thirty years, including the subject horse, Spectacular Bid. He resides in Columbia, Maryland.

Forthcoming titles
in the

# THOROUGHBRED
# Legends

series:

## John Henry

## Personal Ensign

## Sunday Silence

## Ruffian

Available titles

## Man o' War

## Dr. Fager

## Citation

## Go for Wand

## Seattle Slew

## Forego

## Native Dancer

## Nashua

### www.thoroughbredlegends.com

*Editor* — Jacqueline Duke
*Assistant editors* — Judy L. Marchman, Rena Baer
*Book design* — Brian Turner